Ron Diamond

GWYNNE DYER has worked as a freelance journalist, columnist, broadcaster, and lecturer on international affairs for more than twenty years. Born in Newfoundland, he originally trained as an historian and served in three navies before taking up an academic position at the Royal Military Academy, Sandhurst. In 1973, he gave up his day job and turned to writing and documentary filmmaking. Since then, his major activity has been his twice-weekly column on international affairs, which is published by 175 papers in some forty-five countries and is translated into more than a dozen languages.

Dyer's first television series, the seven-part documentary *War*, aired in the mid-1980's and one episode, "The Profession of Arms," was nominated for an Academy Award. The accompanying book, also titled *War*, won the Columbia University School of Journalism Award in 1986. Dyer's books include *The Defence of Canada: In the Arms of the Empire* (1990), which he co-authored with Tina Viljoen, and the 2003 best-seller *Ignorant Armies: Sliding into War in Iraq*. Gwynne Dyer lives with his family in London.

To Emilia, Jack, Ruby, Jacques, Natasha, Mike,
Catherine, and Isaac, whose future it will be

*

"Terrorism" is what we call the violence of the weak, and we
condemn it; "war" is what we call the violence of the strong,
and we glorify it.

– Sydney J. Harris, "Nations Should Submit to the
Rule of the Law," *Clearing the Ground* (1986)

FUTURE: TENSE

THE COMING WORLD ORDER

GWYNNE DYER

A complete catalogue record for this book can be obtained from the
British Library on request

The right of Gwynne Dyer to be identified as the author of this
work has been asserted by him in accordance with the Copyright,
Designs and Patents Act 1988

First published in Canada in 2004 by McLelland & Stewart Ltd.,
Toronto, Ontario

First published in the UK in 2006 by Serpent's Tail,
4 Blackstock Mews, London N4 2BT
Website: www.serpentstail.com

ISBN: 1-85242-917-8
ISBN-13: 788-1-85242-917-2

Printed by Mackays of Chatham, plc

10 9 8 7 6 5 4 3 2 1

CONTENTS

INTRODUCTION

The United States has lost the war in Iraq, and it is only a question of time before it brings its troops home. But it could be quite a long time, and how long matters very much.

It matters more than whether the local power struggles unleashed by the US invasion eventually deliver Iraq into a full-scale civil war. It even matters more than the possibility that Iraq breaks up and drags the whole Fertile Crescent into a war that radically re-arranges the region's frontiers, although that would surely make for interesting times. It matters so much because unless the US withdraws from Iraq in the next couple of years, and leaves in a way that discredits the whole project for global American hegemony in the eyes of the US public, then other great powers will start organizing and arming to contain the rogue superpower. That is the road back to 1914.

It was always likely that some American strategists would be tempted by fantasies of global hegemony after the collapse of the Soviet Union in 1991. The attractions of such a policy would only have increased as it became clear to them in the course of the later 1990s that the two Asian giants, China and India, were growing so much faster than the US that they would eventually become serious rivals to America in the great-power stakes. Among American strategists who shared this perspective, the most intellectually coherent and politically well connected group were the so-called neo-conservatives, and with George W. Bush's entry into the White House in early 2001, suddenly it was they who were in charge of American defence and foreign policy.

It is doubtful, however, that they would ever have persuaded

American public opinion to back their project for global hegemony without the terrorist attacks on the United States in September of that year. The horrors of 9/11 let them put it into action because they were then able to hide their real strategy (at least from the American public) behind the facade of the "war on terror." So it needs to be said quite plainly. It was never about Iraq. It is not really about terrorism either, although the terrorists are still there. It is about the whole way we run the world.

In this perspective, Osama bin Laden is a bit player, but an indispensable one. He is like one of those cartoon characters who removes just one brick from a wall – and one after another, in an endless, slo-mo domino sequence, every structure in sight collapses into rubble. With one spectacular act of terrorism, he set in motion a process that has undermined the United Nations, the international rule of law, the whole multilateral system of collaboration and compromise that keeps the world relatively safe. He probably does not understand that his actions have put half a century of slow and painful progress in stabilizing the international system at risk, for his frame of reference is very different, but he wouldn't mind a bit if he did understand it.

What really would confuse Bin Laden is the fact that he has become what our Marxist friends used to call the "objective ally" of the Bush administration, whose world-changing ambitions might never have got off the ground without the opportunity that he handed them on September 11, 2001. There is now a symbiotic relationship between the Islamist terrorists and the coalition of interests in Washington that has clambered aboard the "war on terror." Neither side wishes the other to triumph, but both thrive on the confrontation – and they have grown far beyond the original small groups of determined people who dragged the rest of us into this mess. In fact, neither the death of Osama bin Laden nor the fall of the neo-conservatives would necessarily bring a return to normality. The rhetoric of jihads and crusades has grown more familiar, and the number of people whose emotions or career interests have committed them to an apocalyptic confrontation has grown greatly.

It is the far side of bizarre, for both the Islamist and the American projects as originally conceived are doomed to fail. The notion that Islamist revolutionaries will sweep to power all across the Muslim world, Talibanize it, and then wage a victorious jihad against the West is as implausible as the idea that the United States can permanently assume the role of global policeman (or, rather, global vigilante), that other countries will acquiesce in this unilateral declaration of hegemony, and that US voters will be willing to pay the cost in American lives and money over the long term. It's not going to happen: the danger is not that extremists from the margins will dominate the global future, but that they will do enormous damage to our future before they go under.

What is really at risk here is the global project to abolish war and replace the rule of force in the world with the rule of law, the project whose centrepiece is the United Nations. It was mainly an American initiative at the start, some sixty years ago, and today it still commands the support of almost every government on the planet (although the Bush administration has been an exception). It is a hundred-year project at least, for it is trying to change international habits that had at least five thousand years to take root. The slowness of change causes immense frustration, especially given the urgency of change in an era of nuclear weapons, and yet the project continues to enjoy majority popular support in almost every country, including the United States. But it is now under serious threat.

The core rule of the UN is that war, except in immediate self-defence or in obedience to Security Council resolutions, is illegal. The new American strategic policy, post-9/11, asserts that the United States has the right to use military force wherever and whenever it judges necessary. Of course, the United States has used military force against foreigners without Security Council approval before, but this time is different.

The UN is a hundred-year project because it will take at least that long for the great powers to stop yielding to the temptation, from time to time, to impose their will on weaker countries by force. The great powers do understand that a world under the rule of law, where the resort to force has become almost unthinkable by long habit, is also in their own long-term self-interest, because they, too, are vulnerable to destruction if war gets out of hand – but every so often they simply cannot resist "solving" a problem by using their own superior force.

The UN system recognized from the start that the great powers were the problem: they were given vetoes precisely so that the Security Council would never find itself in the hopelessly compromised position of trying to enforce the law against them. All hope of progress therefore lies with the gradual habituation of the great powers to obeying the new international law that forbids a unilateral resort to force – and since that is ultimately in their interest too, they have generally at least tried to cloak their actions in legal justifications acceptable to the UN. But current American strategic doctrine *requires* the destruction of the international law embedded in the United Nations Charter.

To believe that this huge shift of doctrine is really driven solely by the "terrorist threat" is about as sensible as believing in fairies. Its real origins lie in the hubris that followed America's "victory" (as the veterans of the Reagan and the first Bush administrations in 1980–92 tended to put it) in the old Cold War. With no Soviet Union to oppose it any more, the United States seemed free to reshape the world in its image if it chose to use its power. But the men and women later known as neo-conservatives who had served those administrations, and who dreamt of exploiting that victory to build a world more congenial to American tastes and interests, were rudely expelled from power in the 1992 election and spent the next eight years in the political wilderness. By the time they returned to office after George W. Bush's election victory in 2000, their initial optimism about the potential transformation of the world through the exercise of American power had been somewhat tempered by their growing awareness of China's emergence as a great power that would one day rival the United States in strength. But that just reinforced their conviction that America had to seize the initiative.

The key to understanding the neo-conservatives is not their politics, a familiar blend of Wilsonian idealism, American exceptionalism and neo-liberalism in amounts that vary from one individual to another, but their shared deep commitment to the traditional strategic world-view. Like quite a large proportion of the American military and foreign policy elite, people like Vice-President Dick Cheney, Defence Secretary Donald Rumsfeld and Secretary of State Condoleezza Rice have been immersed, steeped, utterly marinated in the concepts of classic strategic thought, and they make their plans and conduct their policies as though nothing vital had changed in the world since the 19th or even the 18th centuries: the world is still a battleground on which the great powers contend for superiority, and the game will never end. They bring a sense of moral purpose to the game that would have puzzled the game's master strategists of earlier times, but apart from that they would have been quite comfortable working for Count Bismarck or even Cardinal Richelieu. (Whether they would actually have been hired by either of those men is, of course, a different question.)

Everything that classic strategy teaches the neo-conservatives about the workings of the world adds to their conviction that international institutions and cooperation between the great powers are transient and unreliable guarantees of safety and that the only permanent reality is power. They find themselves in charge of the greatest power of the age, and their first, last and only instinct is to do everything possible to preserve and extend that power. That task necessarily includes sweeping aside obstacles like international institutions and laws that constrain the free exercise of American power, which is the only true guarantor of peace, freedom, democracy, the free market and all the other values they cherish. (They really do, you know. Not one of them gets up in the morning and asks him or herself "What evil deed can I do today?" With the possible exception of Dick Cheney.) So their real goals, all justified in the name of peace, freedom, etc., are to cripple the United Nations, sideline international law, and establish a global free-fire zone for American military power. Plus, latterly, to "contain" China.

The problem is that they were never very good strategists, because they had a grossly inflated notion of the effectiveness of American military power and an astounding ignorance about how the rest of the world would respond to an American offer-you-cannot-refuse of benevolent hegemony. In fact, they have already failed. Their flagship project that was intended as the launch-vehicle for Pax Americana, the invasion and transformation of Iraq, has already proved too big a job for the United States armed forces to deliver on. As for getting the rest of the world to fall into line, it responded to the US initiative by rejecting it without hesitation: among the great powers, only Britain agreed to trail along behind the American invaders of Iraq. But for the governments of great powers, the fact of failure and the official acknowledgement of failure may be separated by years, for their ability to deny reality is formidable. And it is this delay between the fact and the acceptance of the fact that now endangers the world.

If the present US strategy of undermining international law and asserting American military hegemony around the planet is quickly abandoned under the pressure of events in Iraq, then normal service will soon be restored internationally and we will get our global project back with only a few dents in it. If the US adventure in unilateralism continues for many more years, other great powers will start taking steps to protect their interests and the UN will start to die. No other major power wants to abandon the project to outlaw war and start back down the road to alliances, arms races, and all the other old baggage, but if the world's greatest power becomes a rogue state they won't have much choice.

If that happens, we have lost a lot.

CHAPTER I

THE STAKES

"In all of American public life, there is hardly a single prominent figure who finds fault with the notion of the United States remaining the world's sole military superpower until the end of time."

– Professor Andrew Bacevich, Boston University

I t is not enough that the United States lose in Iraq. It must be *seen* to lose by the American public, for otherwise the project that lay behind the invasion of Iraq will soon enough be resurrected by some other administration, and not necessarily a Republican one. The reason that the neo-conservatives have been able to get away with their clumsy strategy and transparent lies for so long is that they can depend on a bi-partisan consensus in the American political elite which holds that US military hegemony is good for the planet and good for the USA. Invading Iraq, it turns out, was a very poor way of launching the take-over bid, but only a very visible and comprehensive failure there will deter that broad political-military elite from trying to relaunch the bid for global hegemony from some more promising location a little later.

Although reluctant to admit even to themselves that their Iraqi adventure has failed utterly, the current managers of American strategic policy are well aware of the damage that prolonged US military involvement in that county is doing to popular support at home for their broader project, and they are now trying to extricate US forces from the quagmire without having to acknowledge defeat. The rapid succession of referendums and elections in 2005, like the effort to build an "Iraqi" (i.e. Kurdish and Shia Arab) army capable of containing the insurgency while American troops withdraw, has the same purpose as the similar exercise that the United States conducted in Vietnam under President Richard Nixon in 1969–73.

Nixon was elected in late 1968 on a promise to end the Vietnam War, but he also implicitly promised that he would do so without the appearance of a humiliating defeat for American military power.

Nixon's quest for that elusive objective took almost five years, during which he and his National Security Adviser, Henry Kissinger, bombed North Vietnam flat, engineered the invasion of another country, Cambodia, and incurred fully two-thirds of all the American casualties suffered in Vietnam – all just to create a "decent interval" between the American withdrawal and the subsequent collapse, so that American military power and political prestige did not suffer a public defeat.   Henry Kissinger collected a Nobel Peace Prize for his part in negotiating the Paris peace accord of 1973 that was meant to give the United States that kind of political cover (though his Vietnamese counterpart, Le Duc Tho, had the good taste to refuse his), but it did not actually work. There was public humiliation for the United States anyway in the end, and the scenes on the roof of the US embassy in Saigon in 1975 were far worse than anything that would have happened if Nixon had just pulled US troops out within months of his election victory in 1968.

The risk now is that a similar pattern of behaviour will prevail in Iraq, with the Bush administration pursuing a muddled course that veers from dreams of victory in Iraq to mere hopes of a dignified withdrawal and back again until it runs out of time in 2008. Given the rapid deterioration in American popular support for the war and in the Bush administration's fortunes more generally, this may seem an unlikely outcome, but President Bush is virtually impossible to remove from office before the end of his term no matter how disaffected public opinion becomes, he has a seemingly unshakable faith in the rightness of his actions, and he has shown great loyalty to his subordinates, including those who led him into this misadventure. It is quite imaginable that he could keep the neo-conservatives in office and persist in his present course right down to the end of his term in late 2008, possibly even authorizing incursions into neighbouring countries like Syria or Iran (as Nixon and Kissinger did in Cambodia) in an attempt to alleviate his local difficulties in Iraq.

Nor is it safe to assume that Congress or the broad American public will turn decisively against him before the end of his term, especially if American military casualties in Iraq remain at the current, relatively low level of around a thousand dead a year. Just one terrorist attack on American soil would virtually guarantee that President Bush could go on using the "war on terror" as political cover for the remainder of his term. And as for the elite, Andrew Bacevich's brutal comment is all too true: the strategic perspective that lies behind the neo-conservative project is implicitly shared by almost all senior American politicians, military officers and even academics on both sides of the party divide.

The idea that the United States can remain "the world's sole military superpower until the end of time" is comically over-ambitious, but there it is, embedded in a thirty-four-page document submitted to Congress in September 2002 entitled "The National Security Strategy of the United States." The claim to global hegemony could not be clearer: "The United States will not hesitate to strike preemptively against its enemies, and will never again allow its military supremacy to be challenged." Never again allow its military supremacy to be challenged? The United States has four per cent of the world's population and a larger but declining share (currently about 20 per cent) of the world's economy. It had a budget deficit of more than half a trillion dollars in 2004, and a foreign trade deficit of about the same size. How is it going to do that?

Obviously, it can't. Sooner or later the American dollar, already seriously overvalued, will crumble under the strain. Sooner or later American voters themselves will pull the plug on the project to turn the United States into the world's policeman (or more precisely, the world's judge, jury and executioner), as the cost of *Pax Americana* in American lives and in higher taxes becomes clear to them. But the dollar's high-wire act could go on for years, since a great many non-American players would also take a severe beating if it suddenly collapsed, and American voters don't even get another chance to vote in a presidential election until late 2008. It could be 2009 or later before the search for the decent interval even gets properly underway – and by then the rest of the world would be a place that had changed drastically for the worse.

If a decisive American defeat in Iraq takes another three, four or five years, huge and maybe irreparable damage will have been done to the international institutions that are our fragile first line of defence against a return to the great-power wars that could destroy us all. We need the United States back as a leading architect of global order, not a hyperactive vigilante, and we need it back now. So, to begin with, how fast could the United States get out of Iraq, and what are the chances that the present holders of power in Washington could disguise a withdrawal as a success?

"The French plan, which would somehow transfer sovereignty to an unelected group of people, just isn't workable."

– US national security adviser
Condoleezza Rice, September 2003

In September 2003, when French president Jacques Chirac urged a high-speed handover of power to Iraqis as the best way of clearing up the huge mess created by the illegal American invasion of Iraq, the US government rejected the idea out of hand. The Coalition Provisional Authority (CPA) that ran the occupation regime under pro-consul Paul Bremer would stay in power as long as necessary to ensure the creation of an Iraqi constitution and the election of an

Iraqi government that was (a) democratic and (b) pro-American.

Coming up with an Iraqi government that matched both of those criteria was a very tall order, given US closeness to Israel and Washington's determination to open the entire Iraqi economy up to foreign companies. In fact, Bremer's predecessor, retired general Jay Garner, had been fired in April 2003 after only a month in the job because he had publicly called for early elections in Iraq; his superiors wanted to privatize the Iraqi economy first, in accordance with a plan that had been drawn up in late 2001. It was a crucial opportunity squandered, but it didn't seem urgent to the new rulers of Iraq at the time.

There had been scattered outbreaks of guerrilla resistance ever since the war officially ended in May, but Bremer's initial response was bluster: "We are going to fight them and impose our will on them and we will capture them or, if necessary, kill them until we have imposed law and order on this country ... We dominate the scene and we will continue to impose our will upon this country." Nobody in Washington panicked, and Deputy Defense Secretary Paul Wolfowitz, ever the unconscious ironist, declared: "I think all foreigners should stop interfering in the internal affairs of Iraq." Even the big car bombs in Baghdad in August 2003 didn't shake the Bush administration's confidence that the CPA was firmly in the saddle and there was no need to rush. But two months later, there was a rush.

"I think we have to recognize that as time goes on, being occupied becomes a problem."

– Paul Bremer, October 2003

By mid-November 2003, the Iraqi resistance had grown from small beginnings – "Bring 'em on," President Bush had confidently said when its attacks began to build up in July – to the point where it was killing an average of three American soldiers a day. Bremer was hastily summoned back to Washington and the policy switched to high-speed "Iraqization": getting Iraqi soldiers and policemen out front as sandbags to protect American troops, which in turn required coming up with a more or less credible Iraqi government that they would be willing to die for. So all of a sudden, handing over "sovereignty" to an unelected group of people stopped being a problem: Washington announced that sovereignty would be handed over to just such a group on June 30, 2004.

They could have been an elected group, of course. Six months was ample time to organize elections in Iraq, and the problem of an out-of-date voters' roll could have been mostly solved by using identity cards and rationing cards. Lots of post-conflict elections have been held in far worse circumstances, and the security situation in Iraq was still manageable in early 2004. But democracy is a messy and unpredictable business. An Iraqi government with a genuine popular mandate would be an unmanageable entity: it certainly would be no friend of Israel, it would probably reverse the privatization process, and it might just order US troops to leave. So it would have to be an appointed government, at least until after the US election in November 2004 was safely past.

In December 2003, that still seemed to be a viable proposition. In fact, it still seemed reasonable for chief political adviser Karl Rove to plan a triumphant return visit to Baghdad by President George W. Bush. The president's surprise visit to US troops in Iraq at Thanksgiving in November 2003 had been a great media success (although he never left Baghdad airport), and the man who had masterminded Bush's political strategy since Texas days immediately started planning a victory lap for the president in Baghdad at the start of the 2004 presidential campaign.

On June 30, 2004, the Liberator of Iraq would land at Baghdad airport and drive into the city past cheering crowds of grateful Iraqis. He would mount a podium in Firdous Square, where one of Saddam Hussein's ubiquitous statues had been toppled in a staged-for-the-cameras event seen round the world on the day Baghdad fell to US troops in April 2003. His speech would wish the newly appointed Iraqi government every success as it took "sovereign control" of Iraq, and gracefully grant its request that American troops stay in the fourteen "enduring bases" that were already under construction in the country to help ensure the stability of the region. He would congratulate it on its commitment to a future Iraqi democracy and to good relations with Israel. God bless Iraq. God bless America. The crowds in Iraq would cheer, the audience in the United States would feel a warm glow of satisfaction, and whatever sacrificial lamb the Democrats had found to run against Bush would change his name and move to Mexico.

At the end of 2003, the game plan still seemed plausible if you lived in Washington, not in Baghdad, for the first crisis of the occupation was past. The pace of the attacks on American troops and on Iraqis who worked for the occupation regime had dropped off after the capture of Saddam Hussein in December, and both the Pentagon and the local occupation authorities in Iraq insisted that they were only the work of scattered Baath Party "dead-enders" and "foreign terrorists" who had infiltrated into the country. By next summer the resistance would be a thing of the past. So Rove pulled the appropriate strings, and in December 2003 the North Atlantic Treaty Organization (NATO) summit that had originally been scheduled for Istanbul in May 2004 was abruptly postponed to the end of June, which happily coincided with the recently announced date for the "handover" of sovereignty in Iraq. If the president were already in Istanbul, only ninety minutes' flying time from Baghdad, on the day before the scheduled handover on June 30, then a surprise visit would work perfectly once again. But it didn't play out quite as Karl Rove intended.

At first, the confident assurances of Donald Rumsfeld at the Pentagon and of Paul Bremer in Baghdad seemed to have some basis in reality. In February and March, Bremer won a major confrontation with the senior religious authority in the Shia community, seventy-three-year-old Grand Ayatollah Ali al-Sistani, who was objecting to the indefinite postponement of elections as a trick devised to cheat Shias out of the democratically elected majority government that was their due. (Shias are 60 per cent of Iraq's population, but have traditionally been dominated by Sunnis.) But Sistani's only weapon was a threat to declare a Shia uprising, which entailed the risk of influence flowing away from him to younger and more radical Shia clerics, so he really had no weapon at all. Eventually, he accepted the US plan to hand over "sovereignty" to an appointed body of Iraqis in June in return for the promise of elections in 2005. Attacks by the Iraqi resistance were rapidly building up again, however, and the CPA seemed to have not a clue as to who was behind them. Then, in April 2004, Iraq exploded again.

There were two triggers, and they were both pulled by Bremer. The first was his complicity in the US military's decision (possibly driven from the Pentagon or even the White House) to besiege the city of Fallujah, whose 300,000 inhabitants were the most defiant supporters of the resistance in the whole of the "Sunni triangle" west and north of Baghdad. On March 31, four US "contractors" (paramilitary security personnel) were killed in their car by members of the resistance in Fallujah. It was not all that uncommon an event in Iraq by the spring of 2004, but a mob of local citizens screaming hatred of the United States then set the dead men's bodies afire and kicked their heads off while others videotaped them. Two of the bodies – headless, handless, and footless – were hung above the stream of traffic crossing the Euphrates bridge and left there for hours. It was a ghastly display, but the reaction of the US forces in Iraq was foolish beyond belief. They besieged Fallujah, and announced that they would seize and occupy it unless the residents handed over those guilty of the atrocity against the contractors.

Sir Jeremy Greenstock, a career diplomat who served as British envoy to the CPA for a time in early 2004 before resigning in despair, said that Paul Bremer should have had a sign on his desk that read: "Security and jobs, stupid." The US military in Iraq should have had one that read: "Hearts and minds, stupid," but instead they gave the resistance more than it could ever have hoped for: a full-scale military siege of an Iraqi city full of young men who were eager to fight, and of old people, women, and children who would inevitably do most of the dying.

"What is coming is the destruction of anti-coalition forces in Fallujah," said Lieutenant-Colonel Brennan Byrne, commander of the 1st Battalion, 5th Marine Regiment. "They have two choices: submit or die." It was never imaginable that the Iraqi militants would hand over the people who had abused the Americans' bodies (if they were even in Fallujah any more), so the US forces were effectively committed to the street-by-street conquest of a middle-sized Iraqi city. That would involve significant American casualties, and a huge toll of deaths and injuries among the civilian population.

The other trigger Bremer pulled, apparently as a free choice, was his decision to close a small-circulation weekly newspaper (less than 10,000 copies) that supported radical Shia cleric Moqtada al-Sadr and to issue a warrant for his arrest. The paper inveighed against the American occupation and printed truth, rumours, and flat lies with a fine lack of discrimination, but in that it differed little from dozens of other weekly party papers that had sprung up in post-Saddam Baghdad. Sheikh Moqtada al-Sadr himself was a more serious proposition: young, radical, and relatively poorly educated in Islamic law, but able to trade on his renown as the son of a revered grand ayatollah who had been murdered by Saddam Hussein – and in charge of a private militia called the al-Mahdi army that drew its recruits from the overwhelmingly Shia slums of eastern Baghdad. Faced with the threat of disappearing into Abu Ghraib or some other part of the US prison system, he mobilized his militia and took over the Shia holy cities of Najaf and Karbala south of Baghdad. If the United States wanted to arrest him, it would have to fight its way into those cities and violate the holy shrines.

American firepower meant that it was possible to capture both Fallujah and the rebel Shia cities without suffering large US casualties, but it could not be done without inflicting huge Iraqi casualties. For a week or so, the offensive against Fallujah was pursued vigorously on the ground, killing at least six hundred residents, most of them civilians. But a large proportion of the local men joined the active resistance, and it became clear even to the US planners that the full subjugation of the city would involve killing thousands of Iraqis and losing a considerable number of their own soldiers. (Twenty- or fifty-to-one kill ratios are quite normal when highly trained soldiers backed by modern artillery and air power take on untrained and poorly armed volunteers fighting amid their own homes, but 138 US soldiers still died in Iraq in April 2004, more than during the war itself.)

The kill ratio was even more one-sided in the Shia cities, where hundreds of members of the Mahdi militia, mostly poor young men from east Baghdad, were killed by American forces on the outskirts of Karbala, Najaf, and neighbouring Kufa with almost no American casualties, mostly by air strikes. US troops never tried to penetrate to the centre of the holy cities for fear of damaging the sacred mosques and completely alienating the Shias of Iraq, who had hitherto been less active in the resistance. Even so, the images being disseminated across the Muslim world were disastrously bad for the United States, as they were almost identical to the images of Israeli troops suppressing resistance in occupied Palestinian towns and cities. Eventually, Washington realized that it would have to back away from both confrontations, and negotiations began to allow it a face-saving way out.

Even worse images began to appear in late April, as the photographs of Iraqis under torture taken by American soldiers at Abu Ghraib prison began to leak out to the media and the public. The obsession with the sexual humiliation of naked Arab males seemed calculated to confirm all the worst imaginable stereotypes that Muslims hold about American behaviour and values, which might just have been an unfortunate coincidence – or it might have been an intrinsic part of the process, for humiliating prisoners and photographing the results are a standard part of the package of measures for putting pressure on captives that is generally known as "torture lite." How much of this behaviour towards the thousands of Iraqis held without charge in US–run prisons was authorized by American military authorities, and how high the blame went, will probably not be admitted for years, but in a sense it does not matter. The result was to blacken the already poor reputation of the United States virtually beyond repair, at least for this generation, in the Arab world.

In the midst of these events, various Iraqi resistance groups began to employ the new tactic of kidnapping and killing civilian foreigners, tens of thousands of whom had arrived in Iraq to work for the many foreign companies that had been granted contracts for the "reconstruction" of the country. A number of these captives were beheaded, their murders videotaped by their killers, and the tapes made available to Arab satellite TV stations or posted on the Web. This led to a general exodus of foreign "carpetbaggers" (to borrow the phrase used during America's own episode of Reconstruction after the Civil War), which caused further major delays in the restoration of basic services like electricity, water, and sewage that had been severely damaged during the American invasion and the subsequent orgy of looting.

The events of April were as much a psychological turning point in the Iraq War as the Tet Offensive of 1968 had been in the Vietnam War. By mid-May, when the worst of the uprisings had abated, the inability of the United States to control the situation by force had become clear to Iraqis and to the world. The US Marines besieging Fallujah were withdrawn and the city was handed over to the nominal control of a Saddam-era Iraqi general who recruited a "Fallujah Brigade" of troops locally, mostly from among the men who had been fighting the Marines – and the city effectively became a no-go zone for foreign forces. Very occasional high-speed drive-throughs by American troop convoys, negotiated well in advance, were permitted by the Sunni resistance forces, but Fallujah became their safe haven and provisional capital.

Farther south in the Shia-majority part of Iraq, Najaf and Karbala also became American-free cities apart from a couple of negotiated patrol routes. Not only had US forces failed to "kill or capture Moqtada al-Sadr" as Lieutenant General Ricardo Sanchez, America's most senior general in Iraq, had loudly vowed to do, but the radical young cleric had gained enormously in prestige and become a serious rival to the more moderate Grand Ayatollah Ali al-Sistani. A CPA opinion poll conducted in May revealed the full extent of the damage: only 2 per cent of Arab Iraqis still saw the Americans as liberators, while 92 per cent saw them as occupiers. A year previously, Iraqi opinion had been almost evenly divided. And a CNN–USA Today poll of 3,500 Iraqis at about the same time found that 57 per cent wanted US and British forces to leave immediately. (Since the 38 per cent who wanted them to stay longer presumably included most Iraqi Kurds, who dream of an independent Kurdistan and therefore prefer a weak and dependent government in Baghdad, among Iraqi Arabs the majority opposing the US presence was probably close to 4 to 1.)

Over May and June, several more cities in the Sunni triangle gained a significant degree of freedom from American forces after ferocious clashes. Ambushes and roadside bombs took a steady toll of American troops while car bombs and kidnappings spread fear among civilians, and it became quite clear that Rove's dream of kicking off President Bush's re-election campaign with a television extravaganza in Baghdad marking a "handover of sovereignty" to a group of unelected Iraqis would have to be cancelled. Even choosing that group of Iraqis became a troubled issue. In mid-May, Ezzedine Salim, the chairman of the existing, virtually powerless Iraqi Governing Council that had been appointed by Bremer the previous year, was killed by a car bomb at the entrance to the Green Zone, the vast American military and civil headquarters area in central Baghdad. Hussein al-Shahristani, the non-partisan scientist selected to be prime minister by United Nations envoy Lakhdar Brahimi, who had been brought in to lend a veneer of legality to the proceedings, either refused to work for the Americans or was rejected by them. (Accounts differ, but Brahimi was heard to mutter, "I'm sure he doesn't mind me saying that Bremer is the dictator of Iraq. He has the money. He has the signatures. Nothing happens without his agreement in this country.")

The man who was eventually selected as prime minister, Iyad Allawi, was a former exile and long-standing CIA "asset" who openly admitted having taken money from fourteen foreign intelligence agencies – all in the cause of overthrowing Saddam Hussein, he insisted, and it may well have been true, but it was not exactly the CV you would choose for a man who had to win the support of a country that was drifting towards a general revolt against its American occupiers. Allawi picked more than half the members of his new cabinet from the former, US–nominated Iraqi Governing Council (on which sixteen of the twenty-five members were returning exiles), but the "handover" (minus President Bush) didn't even take place on June 30 as planned. The resistance forces staged an extravaganza of their own on June 25, carrying out simultaneous attacks on police stations and army barracks in five cities that killed 85 people and injured 320 – so the occupation authorities secretly moved the date for the "transfer of sovereignty" up by two days to avoid the similar round of attacks they feared was being planned for the scheduled date. The actual ceremony was held in a featureless room in the heart of the Green Zone, behind four rings of checkpoints, on the morning of June 28. Most of the witnesses were foreign journalists and American troops.

And nothing changed. There were still 138,000 US troops in Iraq, and it was still true that Iyad Allawi would be dead in a day without their protection. The resistance forces kept attacking, and they were still overwhelmingly Iraqi despite American propaganda: only 2 per cent of the 8,500 "security detainees" arrested by US troops and held in jails at Abu Ghraib or elsewhere were non-Iraqis, and half of those were Syrians from clans that straddle and habitually ignore the border between the two countries. American troops and the Iraqi soldiers and police who had been recruited to help them kept on getting killed at about the same rate as before: American military deaths in Iraq passed the thousand mark in the late summer of 2004. Iraqi civilians kept dying from car bombs, crime, and American firepower alike: recorded deaths from gunfire in Baghdad were up ninety-fold from Saddam's time, and many more were unrecorded.

The next major upsurge of the resistance in Iraq, after the peaks of November 2003 and April 2004, came in August 2004, when the militia of the radical Shia cleric Moqtada al-Sadr again took control of the Shia holy cities of Karbala, Najaf, and Kufa. American forces spent most of a month killing the poorly armed Shia militiamen, eventually penetrating within a hundred feet of the Imam Ali shrine in the centre of Najaf, but again they finally drew back from attacking the mosque itself. Al-Sadr's surviving militiamen marched out, still armed, after mediation by Grand Ayatollah Ali al-Sistani. At least a thousand militiamen and civilians had been killed, but al-Sadr emerged from the confrontation stronger, and the US–approved government of Iyad Allawi emerged weaker.

Meanwhile, most of the cities of the "Sunni triangle" slid inexorably into the grip of the resistance: not just Fallujah, but Ramadi, the whole of Anbar province, and cities like Samarra. The "Fallujah Brigade" fell apart, the National Guard battalions that had originally been allowed to operate in those cities were decapitated (sometimes literally), and US forces retreated to fortified encampments on the edge of the desert. In November, when the US presidential election was safely past, a large US force conquered Fallujah by the simple expedient of ordering all civilians to leave and killing anyone who remained, but it had no perceptible result in terms of fewer guerrilla attacks elsewhere.

In January 2005 the long-delayed elections for an Iraqi parliament were finally held, with the predictable result that most Kurds voted for the main Kurdish party, most Shia Arabs gave their votes to a coalition of religious parties blessed by Ayatollah Sistani, and most Sunni Arabs boycotted the polls. It took more than three months to cobble together a Shia-dominated coalition with the Kurds, because the US had written the voting rules in such a way that a new government had to receive the votes of two-thirds of the parliament's members. (This was intended to ensure that the Kurds would have to be included in any coalition, where they would be able to block any demand for early American withdrawal from Iraq.)

The government that finally emerged in early May 2005, headed by Prime Minister Ibrahim al-Jaafari, a leading Shia politician, had no control over the operations of American forces on Iraq soil, no authority over what still amounted to a separate Kurdish army in the north, and no credible representation from the Sunni Arab community, most of which continued to support the insurgency. American military casualties had been contained – less than a hundred dead in most months – by pulling most US patrols off the streets and handing the task over to the (almost entirely Shia and Kurdish) new Iraqi army that was being trained by the United States, but Iraqi casualties soared. About 750 Iraqis were killed in May 2005, the great majority of them members of the army and police forces that were collaborating with the US occupation. Whatever hopes there had been that elections might put an end to the resistance had come to naught – so was Iraq turning into another Vietnam?

There were already more American troops in Iraq in May 2005 than there had been in South Vietnam in 1964, just before President Lyndon Johnson began the escalation that eventually put a half-million American troops on the ground in that country. The Iraqi guerrillas and "terrorists" they faced – a distinction without a difference; all guerrillas use terrorist methods – were less united than the Viet Cong had been in South Vietnam and they did not have a North Vietnam to back them up, but they were managing to cooperate against the occupiers and they had the sympathy of the whole Arab world. And President Bush didn't really have the option of following President Johnson's example and flooding Iraq with troops.

By scraping the bottom of the barrel, Bush would be able to find around another twenty or thirty thousand troops for Iraq, for a total of 160–170,000 – but after that he would have to bring back the draft, which would have been political suicide. Besides, escalating the war hadn't solved the problem for Lyndon Johnson: even with 550,000 American soldiers and 450,000 South Vietnamese troops available, the United States had been unable to defeat the guerrillas in a country with a smaller population than Iraq. What the United States was up against in both countries, behind the screen of ideological cant about communism or Islamism, was nationalism, and once a majority of local nationalists had decided that America's motives for being in their country were not good – whether they were or not – then the game was hopeless. That point had already passed in South Vietnam by 1964, although the US military involvement there lasted another nine years, and it had already passed in Iraq by the summer of 2005.

"Television brought the brutality of war into the comfort of the living room. Vietnam was lost in the living rooms of America – not on the battlefields of Vietnam."

– Marshall McLuhan, 1975

In anti-colonial guerrilla wars, the locals always win. The Dutch learned that lesson in Indonesia, the French in Vietnam and Algeria, the British in Kenya and Cyprus, and the Portuguese in Angola and Mozambique. The United States went through the same learning process in Vietnam, and the Russians in Afghanistan. It's all about how much time and how many lives the two sides are willing to spend on the issue. The fighting may go on for years, the better-equipped foreigners will win almost all the battles, and ten or twenty guerrillas may die for each foreign soldier, but there is an endless supply of locals and very little patience for a long war with high casualties back in the foreigners' home country. In the end the foreigners invariably succumb to the temptation to cut their losses and go home, because otherwise there will be no end: the guerrillas are never going to quit and go home, because they already are home. And it makes no difference how noble the foreigners think their motives are; only the opinion of the locals counts.

Almost all of America's friends and allies in the world understand this, which is why they have been trying to make it easy for the United States to get out of Iraq quickly without losing too much face. That was the real purpose of the Security Council resolution in June 2004 that retrospectively cast a cloak of legitimacy over the US presence in Iraq and the puppet regime it was installing there. French president Jacques Chirac, as blunt as ever, called it "an exit strategy from a crisis," but he supported it too.

Nobody was willing to send more troops into the Iraqi cauldron or to bless the occupation as a UN operation – the whole point of the exercise was to get the US troops out – but they were all willing to indulge in a little hypocrisy if it would speed American troops on their way. They were well aware that chaos might reign in Iraq afterwards, but Iraq was in chaos already. The priority for the whole world was to get the US defeat in Iraq over with and forgotten as soon as possible and with the least possible damage to American self-esteem, rather than submit to the inevitability of a long, bitter, losing guerrilla war that would set the United States against the rest of the world, feed Islamist extremism, and undermine the whole project for great-power collaboration in the service of peace.

It is not clear, however, whether many senor figures in Mr Bush's party or even in the Democratic Party have even yet fully grasped the fact that the Iraq adventure has already failed, and that the only sensible course that remains is to declare a victory and leave as soon as possible. Pride, and the myth of American military strength, bulk large in the calculations of the political elite, for whom "failure is not an option." The belief that American ingenuity and determination can overcome any obstacle was the reason that the Vietnam War went on long after rational decision-makers would have cut their losses and left, and the same fatal flaw may now be at work in Iraq.

The main argument that is now offered against an early

American withdrawal from Iraq is that it would abandon the country to a civil war, but this is a highly questionable rationale. True, Iraq is an ethnically complex country that has suffered under a succession of bad governments, and the dominant political tradition at the top since the overthrow of its British-imposed monarchy in 1958 has been brutally simple: losers die. However, all the other countries in the vicinity are ethnically complex too: Turkey is almost a quarter Kurdish, Syria has Sunni Arabs and Alawites and Druze and Kurds, Lebanon omits the Kurds but adds several varieties of Christian Arabs to the mix – and Iran has Persians and big minorities of Kurds, Azeri Turks, Arabs, Turcomans, and Baluchis. Most of these countries also have turbulent and frequently violent political histories, and all of them have seen clashes between ethnic groups in the past century. But only one of them, Lebanon, has tumbled into a full-scale civil war. There is no particular reason to believe that Iraq would do so if American forces left. It didn't during eight decades of independence before the United States invaded.

There is not even any good reason to despair of a democratic future for Iraq, provided that American troops do not stay so long that power automatically devolves to the men with the guns who finally drive them out. If Turkey is a fully democratic country and Iranians keep trying to turn their country into one, why can't Iraqis do the same?

Yet there is reason for pessimism about the likelihood of an early US exit from Iraq. The Islamist radicals associated with the al-Qaeda network would certainly do their best to prevent it. Ever since 9/11, the Bush administration has been doing exactly what they want, invading Muslim countries and serving as an unpaid but highly effective recruiting agent for the extremists across the whole of the Muslim world. Back in 2001, popular support for the Islamists was in decline almost everywhere except Saudi Arabia and perhaps Pakistan. Even in Afghanistan, where the Taliban were actually in power, the incessant meddling of the Islamists in the details of private life was making them almost as unpopular as the communists had been, for much the same reasons. The US invasions of Afghanistan and Iraq have given the Islamists an enormous boost in the Muslim countries that are their main targets (just as the planners of 9/11 intended), and they will try to keep American troops mired in the Middle East for as long as possible. At the moment, however, they don't have to put a lot of effort into it.

It is hardly surprising that there has not been a single act of terrorism sponsored by Islamists on US territory between September 12, 2001, and the time when I write this in late 2005. Apart from one bumbling British convert to Islam, Richard Reid (who dropped the matches while trying to light the explosive soles of his shoes on a flight from Paris to New York), there has not been even one serious attempt to attack Americans on or near home soil – if indeed the mentally disturbed Reid was operating under direct orders from al-Qaeda. This absence of attacks may, of course, be thanks to the eagle-eyed efficiency of the CIA, the FBI, the DIA, the NSA, MI5, MI6, GCHQ, CSIS, and all the other intelligence services, but a likelier explanation is that such attacks have not been ordered. The Bush administration is already doing what al-Qaeda wanted; why risk discrediting it by making further terrorist attacks in the United States?

On the other hand, if Bush were to show serious signs of intending to pull out of Iraq, al-Qaeda would promptly stage the largest attack it could manage on US soil in an attempt to seal the exit shut. There will be no early withdrawal of American troops from Iraq – nor of British troops either. And in the British case, at least, there is no deeper strategic motive underlying the prime minister's publicly stated rationale for keeping British troops in Iraq. He really does believe what he says.

"Let us be clear what is happening in Iraq. It is the battle of seminal importance for the early twenty-first century. It will define relations between the Muslim world and the West ... Who is trying to bomb the UN and Red Cross out of Baghdad? Or killing Iraqi civilians in terrorist attacks? Or sabotaging the work on electrical cables or oil installations? Not America. Not Britain. Not the coalition. But Saddam's small rump of supporters, aided and abetted by foreign terrorists.

"And why are they doing it? Because they agree with me about this battle's importance. They know that if we give Iraq democracy, set it on a path to prosperity, leave it in the sole charge and sovereignty of the Iraqi people ... it means ... the death of the poisonous propaganda monster about America these extremists have created in the minds of much of the world."

– British prime minister Tony Blair, November 10, 2003

Like his nineteenth-century predecessor William Ewart Gladstone, Tony Blair can "convince most people of most things, and himself of almost anything," but the notion that the future domestic political arrangements in Iraq are of great moment to the rest of the world is just fantasy. Nevertheless, the invasion of Iraq, and how long the occupation lasts, *is* of great moment, because, for the United States at least, Iraq is the linchpin of a far larger enterprise. The point where things began to go badly wrong in the world was not 9/11, which was the sort of isolated tragedy that happens from time to time, with a death toll on the same scale as a small battle, a medium earthquake, or a minor flu outbreak. The real turning point was January 29, 2002, when President George W. Bush gazed earnestly into the teleprompter and told us all in his State of the Union message that he was declaring war on the "axis of evil." Suddenly he was Ronald Reagan, and it was the Cold War again.

Even the old vocabulary came back: Bush constantly referred to the "Free World" in his public statements, as if it were still 1984. The "war on terror" was another global crusade against evil, with everybody expected to fall in behind American leadership, and it would go on indefinitely: permanent low-level war, worldwide, just like in the Good Old Days. We were all caught up in a fantasy rerun of America's Finest Hour, and the question is: Why?

"On 16 September 1985, when the Commerce Department announced that the United States had become a debtor nation, the American Empire died."
                                                    – Gore Vidal, 1987

Most of the full-blown conspiracy theories have as their point of departure the extreme vulnerability of the American economy. US foreign trade went into deficit in the 1970s and never recovered; in recent years, the American trade deficit has ballooned to half a trillion dollars a year. To make matters worse, the US federal government has been running enormous deficits most of the time since the Republicans discovered fiscal irresponsibility under President Reagan in the 1980s. There was a successful attempt to move back to balanced budgets under Bill Clinton in the mid-to-late 1990s, but under George W. Bush the annual budget deficit attained a new record of more than half a trillion dollars within two years.

Normally, huge budget deficits cause roaring inflation, which forces central banks to raise interest rates and rein in the rampant government borrowing (at the expense of killing growth in the rest of the economy as well). Normally, too, an enormous foreign trade deficit will cause the external value of the currency to drop like a rock, forcing the guilty government to slash imports – and, once again, to jack up the local interest rate in an attempt to attract foreign funds and stabilize the currency. But in the United States, none of these things has happened. The entire economy is sustained by an inflow of foreign capital so enormous that it covers the entire trade deficit and also, one way and another, the budget deficit.

It is the Indian Rope Trick conducted on a national scale. Well-to-do Americans reward themselves with massive tax cuts, the government goes on spending like there is no tomorrow – and the party will never have to end so long as foreigners, almost all of them in Europe or east Asia, are willing to keep pouring their money into the United States. Why do they do that, and is there any risk that they might stop?

They do not do it for the allegedly higher returns available in the US stock market: a third of the inflow of foreign capital goes straight into relatively low-yielding bonds, and most of the rest into blue chips. They do it because they see the United States as the safest place to park their money. It is the centre of the world economy, after all, and the dollar is the world's reserve currency. But there is a dangerous circularity to this argument: the foreigners go on investing because the US economy is strong, and it remains strong only because they continue to invest. What if one day the huge budget deficit caused the confidence of the foreign investors to falter? It would suddenly become clear that the emperor is wearing no clothes – and the sky would fall.

In mid-2004, the total amount of foreign money invested in the United States in forms that could be sold off fairly quickly was $8 trillion. If those investments started to move out, the US dollar would fall so fast that the dollars that moved on Day Two of the panic might be worth only half as much in euros or yen as the dollars that moved on Day One. Nobody would win in such a panic, neither Americans nor foreigners, so the latter have almost as great an interest in pretending that the emperor is fully clothed as the former. Nevertheless, the markets have a way of discovering the truth sooner or later: the US dollar's steady fall since the beginning of 2003 has already inflicted such losses on exporters who denominate their prices in dollars (like the oil producers) that its continued status as the world's main reserve currency, used for most international transactions, is becoming doubtful.

The US economy is a confidence trick based on everybody else's perception that the United States is centrally important for the world's security and that its economy is equally central in the global economy. Both those propositions were true in 1945; neither is actually true any more.

The post–Second World War recovery of the European economies and the subsequent extraordinary growth of the East Asian economies have shifted the centre of gravity of the global economy back to Eurasia, now home to about three-quarters of the world's gross domestic product (GDP). The United States still has the biggest single economy, but it is separated by wide oceans from all the others and there is no non-historical reason why it should still be seen as central.

The political and strategic centrality of the United States lasted longer, because until the mid-1980s the core of Eurasia was controlled by communist powers that were fundamentally hostile to both democracy and the capitalist system: the Free World really did face a mortal threat, and depended on America's military strength (above all its nuclear weapons) for protection. But China has been a capitalist country for most practical purposes for about twenty years now, and Russia hasn't even been communist for fifteen years, so where's the threat? Why does everybody else need the United States any more? They don't – but if the party is to continue, they must be persuaded that they do.

This is where the conspiracy theories kick in. The earliest to gain wide currency in the United States was the hypothesis that Saddam Hussein had been promoted to Target Number One because he was threatening to re-denominate Iraqi oil exports in euros rather than dollars, a move that might cause other oil producers to follow suit and trigger the collapse of the dollar. A much more elaborate and sophisticated version, now pretty much the industry standard, was offered by Emmanuel Todd in his book *After the Empire: The Breakdown of the American Order,* first published in France as *Après l'empire* in 2002: "There is a hidden logic behind the drunken sailor appearance of American diplomacy. The real America is too weak to take on anyone except military midgets ... These conflicts [Afghanistan, Iraq] that represent little or no military risk allow the United States to be 'present' throughout the world. The United States works to maintain the illusory fiction of the world as a dangerous place in need of America's protection."

In Todd's view, President Bush's declaration of an open-ended "war on terror" of indefinite duration after 9/11, and his subsequent nomination of an axis of evil that must be expunged by American-led coalitions, were actually intended to be a way of reviving the old American global leadership role of the Cold War even though there was no longer a global military threat. America's economic vulnerability could only be disguised by emphasizing its global strategic role, and in the absence of the Soviet Union and the threat of the Third World War, terrorism would just have to fill the bill.

Todd believes that this is essentially a bipartisan policy, pointing out that the United States first began to fixate on "rogue states" and to pump up both the dangers they allegedly posed and its own defence budget under the Clinton administration in the later 1990s. Since US military strength is quite limited in ground forces, and since the American public has a very low tolerance for military casualties, the designated enemies that are first to be inflated as bogeymen and then crushed to demonstrate the indispensability of American military power must be small, weak states that will crumble quickly. This is the phenomenon for which Todd invented the now-famous phrase "theatrical micro-militarism" – and its primary political purpose, he argues, is to make it appear that the United States is shouldering the burden of defending the world from chaos. This applies just as much to Bill Clinton's no-American-casualty, air-attacks-only little wars against Iraq in 1998 (Desert Fox) and Kosovo in 1999, in Todd's view, as it does to Bush's wars post-2001. It was Clinton's secretary of state, Madeleine Albright, who told the *New Republic* in 1998: "If we have to use force, it is because we are America. We are the indispensable nation." And so long as everybody else believes that, the party will continue.

If such a bipartisan and Machiavellian approach to America's difficulties really did exist, then we would all be in very deep trouble, but the evidence for it is less than convincing. First, there is no other way that America *can* fight now: it is politically unimaginable that the United States would ever commit its forces to combat against a first-rate military opponent on the ground, so the pattern of recent American wars proves nothing. Second, the multiple failures of planning, foresight, and strategic calculation that litter the history of both the Clinton and the younger Bush administrations make it very hard to believe that behind it all was a subtle master plan for restoring America's geostrategic position in order to ward off an impending economic crisis that almost nobody in official Washington admits is coming. But we do need to know how long the present foreign policy will last, and how hard the landing will be when the United States finally has to face strategic and economic realities.

Here the argument gets more worrisome, because it no longer depends on a conscious conspiracy. People in positions of power in the United States, faced with the reality of America's declining political importance and its precarious economic situation, have been and will be forced to respond to the problems arising from America's relative decline in strategic importance and economic power in one way or another even if they only dimly understand them – and the course of least resistance, if they are not prepared to make a rigorous analysis and tough choices, will be to drift back towards solutions that served the United States well in the past. The default choice is to recreate the world of the Cold War, or at least a pale facsimile of it, because that was when the United States really was the indispensable nation, with a genuine and legitimate role at the centre of both politics and economics. The orgy of nostalgia that accompanied the death of Ronald Reagan in the summer of 2004 illustrated just how powerful is the longing throughout the US political elite for a return to the halcyon days of the Cold War – and it is a bipartisan longing, because it comes out of the shared historical experience of the present adult generation, regardless of their political ideology.

That means that American administrations of either party will instinctively tend to go for a massive, Cold War–style confrontation as the "solution" to any significant threat that comes along, like terrorism, particularly because that approach will resonate well with an electorate that is more uncomfortable than most with nuance and complexity. But that still does not explain the unprovoked American invasion of Iraq, which had no credible links to anti-US terrorism.

This is where the lesser conspiracy theory comes in. This quite widespread theory argues that the neo-conservatives in the Bush administration simply seized on the opportunity presented by 9/11 to launch their cherished project for *Pax Americana* and put America back in charge of the world where it belongs. They had total confidence in the supremacy of US military power and they hadn't a clue about the vulnerability of what they saw as the American economic miracle. The strongest evidence for this is the fact that the Bush administration pushed through the biggest tax cuts in history, despite the huge US trade deficit and the extreme vulnerability of the US dollar, as if oblivious to the linkage between the health of the US economy and foreign investor confidence. "Reagan proved that budget deficits don't matter," snapped Vice-President Dick Cheney when Treasury Secretary Paul O'Neill protested against the massive tax cuts. (O'Neill later resigned over the issue.)

"The lunatics have taken over the asylum," as the *Financial Times* put it in May 2003, arguing that the "more extreme Republicans" were deliberately trying to engineer a fiscal catastrophe in order to be able to justify an assault on federal aid to the poor: "Proposing to slash federal spending, particularly on social programs, is a tricky electoral proposition, but a fiscal crisis offers the tantalizing prospect of forcing such cuts through the back door."

In this version of reality, the neo-conservatives were thoroughly self-deluded about America's economic strength, but they did have a coherent politico-military strategy and they were doing their best to put it into practice. They had seized upon terrorism as useful domestic cover under which they could get *Pax Americana* up and running – and the invasion of Iraq was their launch vehicle. The world just didn't co-operate, mainly because their assumptions are wrong. Shame about all the lives. That is not a pretty picture, but it would mean that the world's American problem is containable. The United States is not becoming a rogue nation; it just fell temporarily into the hands of a band of ideological adventurers who are not even representative of the older traditions of the Republican Party.

There is also another possibility, which is that the people controlling defence and foreign policy in the Bush administration just blundered into Iraq because they really believed their own propaganda about weapons of mass destruction and an Iraq–al-Qaeda link, even though people with no access whatever to secret intelligence and just a little common sense knew that it was patent nonsense. The invasion of Iraq was simply a mistake, and they'll try to do better next time. This is very much the option to be preferred, but it doesn't really have the ring of truth to it.

So there you have it. The more radical conspiracy theorists argue that there is a conscious and very sophisticated strategy, tacitly shared by both the Republican and the Democratic wings of what Gore Vidal calls the Property Party, to preserve American global hegemony and the illusion of US economic indispensability in the much less favourable environment of the post–Cold War era. Iraq, in this strategy, would be seen by the mainstream political elites on both sides in Washington as a useful tool to that end. Others, reading the documents produced by the Project for a New American Century over the years, would narrow the focus and say that the Iraq adventure was really the opening move in a hare-brained plan for global domination hatched by a tight little band of neo-conservatives who staged a successful takeover of the traditional Republican Party. Or was it just an isolated, horrible mistake by a group of arrogant people who knew a great deal less than they thought they did?

Cock-up or conspiracy? The answer matters a great deal, because there is so much more at stake now than just the future of Iraq or the Middle East.

If American troops are home from Iraq a year from now and the idea of American global hegemony has lost favour in Washington, then we get the world of the late 1990s back relatively undamaged, and we can pick up from where we left off with the job of building the multilateral institutions that we need to see us through the international storms that are sure to come. This is still a world where almost all the bigger countries have nuclear weapons, and our task is to use the "holiday from history" that we have been granted since the beginning of the 1990s to strengthen the international rule of law and the habits of co-operation among the great powers now that they are not (at least for the moment) enemies. It could work, if we have enough time before climate change and the rise of new great powers and all the other pressures that we know are on the way overwhelm us.

It will not work if the United States stays in Iraq. If that happens, sooner or later most of the other great powers will give up on the United Nations and the rule of law in favour of getting together to counterbalance the weight of the rogue superpower, and the drift back into the bad old world of alliances and confrontations will have begun. Especially it will not work if the United States really is pursuing a coherent strategy of redefining the world in terms of a perpetual, global "war on terror" with itself as leader: that simply will not fly elsewhere, although it sells quite well in the United States at the moment.

Moreover, the isolation and loss of international confidence that the United States will suffer if it continues to pursue this course could easily lead to an early and extremely painful collapse of the dollar, not a gradual decline and a relatively soft landing. Jim Rogers, the Wall Street wizard who in 1973 in partnership with George Soros co-founded the Quantum Fund, one of the first and most successful hedge funds, last year told *The Guardian* that "The US dollar is going the way that sterling went as it lost its place as the world's reserve currency. I suspect there will be exchange controls in the US in the foreseeable future ... We Americans are going to suffer." Most economists who are not on the payroll, so to speak, would agree that America's economic situation is grave. A sudden collapse would inflict such economic hardships on ordinary Americans that it could well lead to a further radicalization of US domestic politics and foreign policy.

The stakes are much higher than they seem. The foundations of the First World War were laid by decisions that were made ten to twenty years before 1914, and after that it was very hard for anyone to turn back. There is a strong case for saying that we have arrived at a similar decision point now; what happens in the next year or so matters a lot, so we need some answers fast. Is the terrorist threat really worth worrying about? Is there a serious bipartisan project for restoring American global hegemony, or is it merely a bunch of neo-conservatives dreaming of lost glories – or is it just the usual cock-up on an unusually large scale?

CHAPTER II

THE ISLAMIST PROJECT

Summoning up every thread of experience and courage, I looked Khalid in the eye and asked: "Did you do it?" The reference to September 11 was implicit. Khalid responded with little fanfare: "I am the leader of the al-Qaida military committee," he began, "and Ramzi is the coordinator of the Holy Tuesday operation. And yes, we did it."

He went on: "About two and a half years before the holy raids on New York and Washington, the military committee held a meeting during which we decided to start planning for a martyrdom operation inside America. As we were discussing targets, we first thought of striking at a couple of nuclear facilities but decided against it for fear that it would go out of control."

I was dumbfounded. Nuclear targets? Could he be more specific?

"You do not need to know more than that at this stage, and anyway it was eventually decided to leave out nuclear targets for now."

"What do you mean 'for now'?"

"For now means 'for now,'" Khalid said, silencing me.

– Yosri Fouda, *Masterminds of Terror* (2003)

L et's start with whether there is really a terrorist threat worth worrying about – *really* worrying about, in the sense that we mobilize all our resources to fight it, change the way we live, invade foreign countries, generally turn our world upside down. The quoted interview (opposite), which took place in April 2002, is taken from a book by Yosri Fouda, chief investigative reporter for the Arabic-language satellite TV channel al-Jazeera; "Khalid" is Khalid Shaikh Mohammed, generally reckoned to be number three in the al-Qaeda organization, and Ramzi, co-ordinator of the Holy Tuesday operation, is Ramzi bin al-Shibh, also quite senior in the organization. Fouda called his book *Masterminds of Terror*, presumably because the marketing department insisted on it, and if you close your eyes you can just imagine these master terrorists in their secret underground lair. It's a bit lower-tech than the headquarters of the typical James Bond villain, but basically the same idea – and from these hidden headquarters, the orders go out to legions of terrorists obedient unto death all around the world.

Well, not quite. The interview actually took place in a safe house in Karachi where Khalid and Ramzi were still kicking their heels eight months after 9/11, having fled Afghanistan after the US–led invasion. The "military committee" was scattered to the winds, and if Khalid was trying to organize further attacks he wasn't having much success: there had been no major Islamist attack since 9/11. Five months after the interview, Ramzi was wounded in a shootout and arrested. Six months after that, Khalid was picked up by the Pakistani police, asleep in a house in a Rawalpindi suburb. They also found his laptop and large numbers of notes littering the room, which gave them hundreds of names, addresses, and telephone numbers to chase. He had clearly not been paying attention back in terrorist school.

Not only are al-Qaeda's "masterminds of terror" not ten feet tall, they are sometimes seriously amateurish. They got very lucky once, on 9/11, because they came up with a way of committing mayhem that no security force in the world had thought to guard against: five-man teams of suicide airplane hijackers that included trained pilots. But that was a once-only surprise, and in all the attacks by al-Qaeda and similarly inclined Islamist groups since then – a night-club in Bali, a synagogue in Tunisia, a hotel in Mombasa, trains in Madrid, the Underground and a bus in London and so on – they have not managed to kill as many people as on that single occasion. The attacks are absolutely standard low-tech terrorist stuff – car bombs, explosives stuffed in backpacks, and the like.

So why have we been hearing about nothing but terrorism for the past four years? Why have there been two wars, in Afghanistan and Iraq, that have killed at least ten times as many people as the terrorists have? If the threat is that small, why are thousands of mostly innocent people in prison on suspicion of terrorism, without charge or prospect of release? Hasn't all this been blown up way out of proportion?

Yes, of course it has. It has been inflated mindlessly by the media, but also quite deliberately by powerful people with political agendas. One way of restoring a sense of proportion is to figure out who the terrorists of al-Qaeda and its various clones and affiliates really are, what their goals and strategy are, and how they fit into their own culture and society: Are they the coming thing in the Muslim world, or an isolated minority of fanatics, or something else entirely?

Another way is simply to figure out the maximum amount of damage they might do.

If we are ever to get our sense of proportion back about terrorism, we need a logarithmic scale for disasters like the one they use for stars. Only the very brightest stars in the sky are First Magnitude; divide the brilliance by ten for Second Magnitude stars, by a hundred for Third Magnitude, and so on. Ranking human disasters by the same system, only those that could kill, say, half the population in question would be First Magnitude. For the twelve million Jews who lived in Europe in 1939, the Holocaust was a First Magnitude calamity: half of them were dead by 1945. At the global level, a First Magnitude disaster would be one that killed around three billion people: it is possible to imagine a return of the Black Death, for example, that would kill three billion people, and an all-out global nuclear war could reach the same casualty level.

Divide by ten, and a Second Magnitude global disaster is one that kills in the low hundreds of millions of people. A "clean" Third World War with relative restraint in the nuclear targeting of cities and no nuclear-winter effects would fall into this range. The AIDS epidemic may ultimately prove to be a Second Magnitude disaster, although a very slow-moving one. Divide by ten again, and we are down to Third Magnitude disasters like the First and Second World Wars and the Spanish influenza outbreak of 1918–19, which all killed 10 to 50 million people. An Indo-Pakistani nuclear war would be a Third Magnitude disaster, as would be an Israeli decision to unleash its nuclear arsenal on its Arab neighbours.

Divide by ten once more, and we are down to Fourth Magnitude events, only one-thousandth as big as First Magnitude ones. Big or long-lasting local wars like Korea 1950–53, Vietnam 1965–73, and Sudan 1983–2003 fall into this range, killing two or three million people. The slaughter in the Great Lakes region of Africa that began with the Rwanda genocide of 1994 and continues today in Eastern Congo probably qualifies by now as a Fourth Magnitude event. An out-of-control nuclear meltdown in a densely populated area or a megaton-range bomb exploded at the right height over a very large city could also cause deaths at a Fourth Magnitude level.

Divide by ten yet again, and we drop to the level of purely local catastrophes like the Lisbon earthquake of 1755, the Krakatoa explosion of 1883, the atomic bombing of Hiroshima in 1945, and the wars in former Yugoslavia in the 1990s, each of which killed in the quarter-million range. Potential Fifth Magnitude calamities in the present include the Big One along the San Andreas fault in California, an average year's famine toll in Ethiopia, or a successful terrorist attack on a major city using a ground-burst nuclear weapon.

Another division by ten, and we drop to Sixth Magnitude events like the war in Iraq in 2003, the 2004 earthquake in Iran, and the Arab–Israeli War of 1967, all of which caused 20,000 to 50,000 fatal casualties. Worst-case scenarios for highly successful terrorist attacks using biological weapons very rarely rise above this level. And a final division by ten brings us down to Seventh Magnitude events like the IRA's war in Northern Ireland from 1969 to 1998, the Second Intifada in Israel/Palestine from 2000 to the present, and the 9/11 attacks on the United States in 2001, all of which have caused in the order of three thousand deaths. About as many Americans die each month from gunshot wounds as died in the Twin Towers, the Pentagon, and United Airlines Flight 93, and those losses, unlike the terrorist attacks, recur every month. So why is terrorism regarded by both the US government and media as the world's number-one problem?

True, the 9/11 deaths all occurred on one day, which gave them an impact far greater than similar numbers of deaths spread over a longer period of time. The fact that the attacks were carried out by foreigners on US soil was profoundly shocking to Americans, who had not experienced such a thing (except for Pearl Harbor) for almost two hundred years. The terrorists' choice of powerfully symbolic buildings reinforced the shock, and the fact that the buildings actually collapsed provided a visual image so striking that nobody who saw it will ever forget it. Nevertheless, it is extraordinary that a Seventh Magnitude event can hijack the entire international agenda for years.

The simple response is to blame the media, and God knows they deserve to be blamed. The greedy sensationalism with which the major Western media greet each new terrorist "outrage" has inflated the danger far beyond its true size in the public's mind, in just the same way as their melodramatic coverage of crime has caused popular anxiety about it to rise steeply in most Western countries even as the actual crime rate has fallen steadily in recent years. Public ignorance about the statistics of risk makes this media manipulation easy: there are heavy smokers who worry about terrorist attacks. But it is also true that terrorists always aim to manipulate the media.

Terrorism is the weapon of the weak. It is a technique that tries to maximize the political impact of relatively minor acts of violence – because that is generally all that such weak groups can manage – through the magnifying glass of media coverage. Indeed, terrorism scarcely existed as a discrete political strategy before the emergence of the popular mass media in the late nineteenth century; as a political technique in its own right, terrorism is overwhelmingly a modern phenomenon. And the most important thing about it is that it is relatively speaking a very *small* threat.

Even the biggest one-day terrorist atrocity ever committed, the attacks on the United States on September 11, 2001, was an event whose huge impact is entirely due to the careful choice of high-visibility targets and reflexive, relentless media promotion of the event. The lives of the other three thousand Americans who died violently that same month in gun-related murders, suicides, and accidents were just as valuable, and they would have been relatively cheap to save compared to the immense cost of the "war on terror." But gun deaths happen singly or in small groups, generally out of camera-shot, and as a routine monthly tragedy they are not newsworthy – so nobody called for a "war on guns" in September 2001. This is not to devalue the tragedy of the Twin Towers, but it *is* to say that the "terrorist threat" is not the major threat of our times.

Even the frantic speculation about terrorists getting their hands on weapons of mass destruction in the aftermath of 9/11 failed to impress people who remembered that we lived for forty years before 1990 with the entirely credible threat of thousands of nuclear weapons exploding simultaneously over every city in the entire industrialized world. That was a really serious threat: the weapons existed, their targets were known, and the buttons could be pushed at any time. If terrorists were someday to get their hands on a nuclear device and explode it in some unfortunate city, it would be a disaster, certainly – but a disaster a full three magnitudes smaller than a real nuclear war. And the terrorists will probably never even manage that.

The other truth that has been largely forgotten in the post-9/11 frenzy is that terrorism is a technique, not an ideology or a country. It is a technique that any group can pick up and use, without distinction of ideology, creed, or cause, and the people wielding it could as easily be fanatical anti-government Americans, Trotskyist Germans, or separatist Tamils as Islamist Arabs. (Indeed, the world's leading suicide bombers are still the Tamil Tigers of Sri Lanka, not any Islamist group.) You don't even have to represent a lot of people or a very popular ideology to make an impact as a terrorist; a small number of people with not-very-popular ideas will do. When small groups of terrorists commit spectacular acts of destruction and get the public's attention, it doesn't mean that they have suddenly become large and powerful groups; just that what they did was widely publicized.

The US government should recognize this, but prefers not to. It says that it has declared war on "terror," but to the extent that it is actually fighting terrorism at all, it is waging a struggle solely against the particular brand of Islamist terrorists who attack American targets. That is a very small enemy, though Washington does everything in its power to pump it up. So we return, therefore, to the original question: How did a relatively limited disaster like 9/11 lead to the huge, system-wide disruption we are now seeing? The best answer is that the terrorist project of the al-Qaeda jihadis has collided with and energized another, far more dangerous project for changing the world: that of the American neo-conservatives. The two groups of would-be world-changers do not collaborate or even communicate, and their goals are largely opposed, but they do feed off each other. Both their projects, as a result, are now up and running.

Why does al-Qaeda want to change the world, and why is there a certain sympathy in the Muslim world for its goals, if not for its methods? There is a back story that explains why Muslims almost everywhere perceive themselves as the chief victims of the past few centuries of world history and the West as the chief architect of their misery. There is also a much more recent narrative of disaster that explains why the Arabs in particular are so filled with rage and despair. What the Islamists bring to this stew of resentment and pessimism is a seductive religion-based analysis of why Muslims have been losing for so long, and a programme of action to turn all that around.

"The indivisibility of any aspect of life from any other in Islam is a source of strength, but also of fragility. When all conduct, all custom, has a religious sanction and justification, any change is a threat to the whole system of belief. Certainty that their way of life is the right one thus coexists with fear that the whole edifice – intellectual and political – will come tumbling down if it is tampered with in any way ... And the problem is that so many Muslims want both stagnation and power; they want a return to the perfection of the 7th century and to dominate the 21st, as they believe is the birthright of their doctrine.

"If they were content to exist in a 7th-century backwater, secure in a quietest philosophy, there would be no problem for them or for us. Their problem, and ours, is that they want the power that free inquiry confers without either the free inquiry or the philosophy and institutions that guarantee that free inquiry ... [T]he tension between their desire for power and success in the modern world on the one hand, and the desire not to abandon their religion on the other, is resolvable for some only by exploding themselves as bombs."

– Theodore Dalrymple, *The Times*, April 15, 2004

Dalrymple is quite right about so-called "fundamentalist" Muslims, who see themselves as being at war with the West and the whole of the modern world. Most Muslims do not, of course, but there are few who do not have an ambivalent relationship with what used to be (and, so far as most of them are concerned, still is) the Christian world.

The intense and sometimes obsessive quality of Islam's emotional relationship with what used to be called "Christendom" and is now "the West" has waxed and waned with time, but it is not just due to the natural hostility between rival religions that both inherited their God from the Jews. In some senses, Islam is the other half of "the West": certainly, the Arab world is the other heir of the classical Graeco-Roman world that the two faiths divided between them long ago.

Between about AD 630 and 730, Arab invaders inspired by the new faith of Islam conquered almost half the territory of the former Roman Empire, which is to say around half of the then-Christian world. (Christianity had become the state religion of the Roman Empire about three hundred years before.) It took some generations to convert the conquered lands thoroughly, but with the exception of Spain, which remained mainly Christian despite eight centuries of Muslim occupation and eventually freed itself, the Christians in the new territories gradually dwindled away to a small minority: under 10 per cent in Egypt, Syria, and Iraq, and even less elsewhere.

The Muslim invasions were quite unlike the Germanic invasions that had already overrun Western Europe. The peoples who conquered Roman Germany, France, England, and Italy were mostly illiterate barbarians who brought a Dark Age in their train, although they were relatively easily converted to the far more sophisticated Christian religion. The Arab conquerors of the Fertile Crescent (what is now Israel and the occupied territories, Jordan, Syria, and Iraq), North Africa, and Spain had lots of fanatical desert horsemen in their armies, but the leaders were literate townspeople from the cities of Arabia, and it was their Muslim religion that prevailed in those lands.

There was no Dark Age in the lands conquered by the Muslims; instead the conquerors preserved many of the best elements of classical civilization and married them to the egalitarian spirit of Islam. And this set the pattern for a thousand years: chronic warfare in the borderlands between the worlds of Islam and Christendom, but in the Muslim heartlands a profound lack of interest in the chaotic affairs of the barbarian Europeans. Even the still-civilized Christian rump of the Roman Empire in the Balkans and Anatolia, latterly known as the Byzantine Empire, was not seen by the Arabs as a cultural equal – and besides, newly Islamized Turkish nomads broke into Anatolia in the late eleventh century and started carving Byzantium up into little Muslim-run principalities.

There was one great interruption to this story of Muslim triumph and Christian ruin, of course: the Crusades. The Christians of Western Europe, their Dark Age now past, decided to have a go at recapturing Jerusalem. It had been a Jewish city for a thousand years, a Christian-ruled city for three hundred years, and a Muslim-ruled city for another four hundred and fifty years. There was no law decreeing that the merry-go-round had to stop, and in 1099 the Crusaders took Jerusalem.

It took almost two hundred years of war for the Arabs of the Fertile Crescent and Egypt to destroy the Crusader kingdoms that sprang up along the eastern coastline of the Mediterranean, but after that they largely forgot about Europe again. (The current rhetorical obsession with Western "Crusaders" in Islamist circles is a deliberate revival for propaganda purposes of a long-dead bogeyman.) And then the advance of Islam resumed: in the fifteenth century, Turkish armies conquered Constantinople (now Istanbul), destroyed what remained of the Byzantine Empire, and surged up through the Balkans. By 1529 a Turkish army was besieging Vienna, right in the heart of Europe. The last Muslim kingdom in Spain had been destroyed about a generation before, but there was no obvious reason yet for anybody in the Muslim world to fear that the long high tide of Islam might be turning. A thousand years of Christian–Muslim relations in five paragraphs – but it helps to explain why Muslims were so deeply shocked when the tide did turn.

In the early sixteenth century, there were three very large and powerful civilizations on this planet that dwarfed all the others. They were all in Eurasia: the Christians of Europe in the west, China and its Confucian satellite cultures in the east, and between them, stretching eight thousand miles from Morocco to Java, Islamic civilization. (Hindu civilization in India, which might have made a fourth, had been largely subjugated by Muslim invaders.) Each of these great civilizations naturally assumed moral superiority over the other two, but in practical terms they were roughly equal in size, wealth, and power. They had been the dominant three for almost a thousand years, and there were no obvious signs that a great change was coming.

For educated Muslims in the Middle East, China was a place so far away that they knew little about it except for its art. Europeans were a lot closer, of course, but those were the old, known neighbours, turbulent and uncultured, and they always lost in the end. They had nothing of value to offer the world, and no sensible person took much interest in them. The real world, where interesting and important things happened, was the Muslim world. And then things started going wrong.

It was quite slow at first – European ocean-going ships showing up off the Muslim-ruled coasts of the Indian Ocean and establishing trading posts backed by cannon-fire during the 1500s, the start of the long Turkish retreat down the Balkans in the late 1600s – but gradually it picked up speed. One by one, the Muslim kingdoms of Asia were extinguished or subordinated to European rule; then in the nineteenth century it was the turn of the Muslims of the Balkans and North Africa; by the early twentieth century all the Muslims of sub-Saharan Africa also found themselves living in European colonies. The roof finally fell in on the Arabic-speaking Middle East, the old heartland of Islam, at the end of the First World War. By 1918, all the wealth and power of the Muslim world were gone and 95 per cent of Muslims were living as the subjects of one foreign Christian empire or another. It was the greatest shock and the deepest humiliation that Muslims have ever experienced, and its echoes still influence behaviours and attitudes in the Muslim world today.

I'm not suggesting that Muslims in great numbers are wandering the streets of Jakarta, Karachi, or Istanbul muttering to themselves in fury over this history. Like other people, most Muslims have no detailed knowledge of the past, and anyway they have their own lives to live right now – but most Muslims are aware that something has gone desperately wrong with history, and that Muslims have suffered terribly as a result. They also know that it was mainly the Christian West that was responsible for this disaster.

There is no need for contemporary Westerners to flagellate themselves with guilt over this past. When Muslims held the whip hand, half of the then-Christian world was conquered and lost forever; it's just history, that's all. But Muslim historical grievances are a good deal fresher than Christian ones – and what hurts even more than the old history is the fact that, although the European empires all collapsed half a century ago, allowing the Muslim countries to regain their independence, Islamic civilization had lost its leading place in the world. There are now no rich, powerful, scientifically advanced, and universally feared and respected Muslim countries. This is probably a transient post-colonial phenomenon, but for Muslims of the present generation it remains a deep and open wound.

How much it hurts, however, depends very much on where you live within the Muslim world. In the big Asian countries where most of the world's Muslims live – Pakistan, India (home to 150 million Muslims), Bangladesh, Malaysia, and Indonesia – resentment about the history is mitigated by the fact that there is now some light showing at the end of the tunnel. Economic growth is promising, a better educated younger generation is rising to power, democracy is becoming the norm (except in Pakistan), and it seems likely that the future will be better than the present. Even in the Middle East, the non-Arab countries are no longer obsessed with the West: the younger generation in Iran are more concerned with getting rid of the dead hand of the 1979 "Islamic revolution" that stifles their lives, and Turkey is a modern, democratic, reasonably prosperous country that is in the queue to join the European Union. Only in the Arab world is the pain of military, political, and economic defeat still acute – because it is still going on.

The Arab world is a disaster area by almost every measure. Even the land itself is eroded, salinated, and worn out by ten thousand years of irrigation agriculture and free-range goats; it is barely able to support the three hundred million people who live on it now – half of whom are under twenty-one. The region's population has doubled since the 1970s, and its youthful profile guarantees many more years of high-speed growth. According to the UN's *Arab Development Report* of 2002, prepared by Arab intellectuals and partly sponsored by the Arab League, half of Arab women are illiterate, the maternal mortality rate is four times that of East Asia, and poverty is omnipresent. Living standards have been falling in most of the larger Arab countries for at least a generation now, as vigorous population growth outstrips feeble economic growth. Science and technology are comatose, research and development are practically non-existent, and, across the whole region, youth unemployment is 30 per cent, the highest in the world. All twenty-two Arab states combined, despite all the oil, have a GDP smaller than Spain's, and the whole Arab world translates only 300 books annually from foreign languages. (Greece, population ten million, translates about 1,500 each year.)

The governments of the Arab states are almost uniformly dreadful: near-absolute monarchies or clapped-out military dictatorships that are oppressive, corrupt, and sometimes very cruel. A majority of them are also in thrall to foreign interests, principally those of the United States. Democracy, common enough in the rest of the Muslim world, is non-existent in the Arab world apart from a couple of timid experiments in power-sharing with elected parliaments by relatively benevolent monarchs in Morocco, Jordan, and a few of the smaller Gulf States. This is the oldest civilized region in the world, and yet across the whole range of measures from birth rates and literacy to economic growth and political freedom it comes in behind every other region except sub-Saharan Africa.

The Arabs themselves tend to blame these disasters on the twin curses of oil and Israel, and there is some truth in that. Possession of about half the world's oil reserves has only guaranteed that the Arab countries suffer endless interventions by more powerful foreigners: as they say only half in jest in Washington, "What is all of *our* oil doing under *their* sand?" The sense of helplessness that this has engendered partly explains the striking shortage of pro-democracy activists and civil society enthusiasts in the Arab world. Rightly or wrongly, people believe that the United States simply will not allow local political changes that would damage its interests. The rest of the explanation for the political paralysis of Arab society has mostly to do with the long fixation on Israel.

The creation of Israel in the very centre of the Arab world in 1948 was a political calamity for countries just gaining their independence after centuries of subjugation, first in the Turkish and then in the British or French empires. It was impossible for them to ignore the appeals of their Palestinian neighbours, but the poorly led and ill-disciplined Arab armies didn't have much chance of beating the highly motivated Israeli forces. It was the first of five successive lost wars for the Arabs, and the result has been a helpless obsession with the dwarf superpower in their midst that has fatally distracted them from their own urgent domestic priorities. Moreover, since Israel is a creation of the West, defended by the United States in particular no matter how it behaves, for many, perhaps most, Arabs the struggle with the West is not really over yet. The bitterness runs very deep, and the surprising thing is not that there are so many extremists in the Arab world willing to use violence against the West, but that there are so few.

An Arab bill of indictment against the West would start with the conquest of North Africa by the French and Italians between 1830 and 1911 and the gradual British takeover of Egypt (which was never reduced to outright colonial status) in the late nineteenth century, but that was just imperialist business as usual, no more outrageous than previous Muslim conquests of Christian lands. The real Arab sense of betrayal starts with the First World War, when the British promised that there would be an independent Arab state in the Fertile Crescent if only the Arabs revolted against their Ottoman Turkish overlords. The Arabs believed those promises, but the British and the French secretly agreed to divide up the territory between themselves in the Sykes-Picot Agreement of 1916, even as Colonel T.E. Lawrence ("of Arabia"), having given Britain's word to the Arabs, was helping to lead the Arab uprising. Lawrence spent the rest of his life consumed by guilt.

What the Arabs got as a reward for their assistance to the winning side in the First World War was not the promised independent state but an exchange of colonial masters. In the place of the Turks, who were at least Muslim, they got British or French overlords. They also got the balkanization of the eastern Arab world, as London and Paris carved the separate countries of Iraq, Syria, Palestine, and Jordan out of the former Ottoman lands. They then subdivided them even further: France separated Lebanon from Syria in 1920, with the intention of creating a loyal state dominated by Maronite Christians to control the Syrian coast. Britain was stuck with the pledge it had made to the Zionist movement in the Balfour Declaration of 1917 to create a "Jewish homeland" in Palestine, a pledge that would ultimately result in the partition of Palestine – although London was deeply reluctant to fulfil that pledge, which it knew would alienate not only its Arab subjects in Egypt, Sudan, Palestine, Iraq, and its Arab allies in the Gulf, but far more importantly the huge Muslim population of the Indian subcontinent.

This is not ancient history for Arabs; it is as vivid as today's news, and practically everybody knows about it. It is also the answer to the plaintive American question: Why do they hate us? Even though Americans had very little to do with the creation of Israel.

The original Balfour Declaration was a cynical deal between a British government, going broke in the middle of a world war, that desperately needed new loans and still believed in the old anti-Semitic stereotype that Jews controlled the world's finances, and Zionists who were willing to play up to that myth in order to extract the promise of a Jewish homeland in Palestine. Once the war was won, the British government did everything it could to renege on that promise too, as it had on its commitment to the Arabs, but it proved much harder to walk away from the Balfour Declaration – partly because there were many more Zionist Jews than Palestinian Arab nationalists in influential positions in the great powers of the West, but also because the looming shadow of the Holocaust, prefigured in the anti-Semitic outrages of the Nazi regime in Germany in 1933–39, made it impossible to dismiss the legitimate fears of European Jews that if they stayed where they were, they would be massacred.

The circle could have been squared, of course, if Britain, France, and countries like the United States and Canada had been willing to accept very large numbers of Jewish refugees, but they weren't. The British authorities vacillated, turning the tap of Jewish immigration to Palestine on and off repeatedly, and the local Arab population, foreseeing that they might one day become a minority in their own country – that indeed it was the stated Zionist ambition to make them a minority – fought back with riots and massacres. (Being effectively colonial subjects of Britain, they had no government or army of their own.) Jews in Palestine organized their own militias and terrorist groups to fight both the Arabs and the British, and the final showdown was only briefly postponed by the

Second World War.

The discovery of the Nazi death camps in 1945 made the creation of Israel a certainty. The major Western countries that had failed to save the millions of European Jews who died in the camps simply had to grant the survivors the Jewish homeland they wanted – and that homeland was not to be in England or New England but in Palestine, so happily it would be the Arabs, not British or American voters, who paid the price. Jewish immigration into Palestine soared in 1945–47, and terrorist attacks on British troops by Zionist extremists like the Stern Gang and Irgun forced London to hand the whole problem over to the newly established United Nations and walk away. The UN, then still an overwhelmingly Western organization (as the rest of the world was mostly still colonies), duly decreed the partition of Palestine between the Jews and the Arabs – and then everybody stood back to watch the war as the surrounding Arab states, themselves only independent for a couple of years, attacked the new Jewish state.

Israel not only won the 1948 war but expanded its borders very considerably beyond those laid down in the UN partition plan. It also used the opportunity (as a new generation of Israeli historians openly admits) to drive most of the remaining Palestinian population beyond the borders that were defined by the end of the fighting, thereby ensuring a large Jewish majority within the frontiers of the new state. And that was only the first of five wars that Israel has fought against its Arab neighbours.

In 1956 it conspired with Britain and France to invade Egypt, although in the end American intervention on Cairo's behalf forced the conspirators to withdraw from the Sinai Peninsula and the Suez Canal. In 1967 Israel launched a pre-emptive attack on Egypt, Jordan, and Syria that ended with the conquest of the old city of Jerusalem, the West Bank, the Gaza Strip, the Golan Heights, and the Sinai Peninsula. In 1973 it was struck by a surprise attack from Egypt and

Syria that was designed to force it into territorial negotiations, and although it regained the upper hand militarily after a few days, it did subsequently respond by making peace with Egypt and giving back the Sinai Peninsula. And finally, in 1982, it invaded Lebanon in an attempt to destroy the Palestine Liberation Organization (PLO), which then had its headquarters in Beirut. The initial attack took Israeli forces all the way to Beirut, and they remained in southern Lebanon for another two decades.

There is nothing shocking or even surprising in this. A new country, set up in a region where it is not welcome, is almost bound to have to fight a few wars to persuade the neighbours that it is there to stay, and it scarcely matters who started which one. The wars, if Israel won them (which it did), were bound to cause great anger and bitterness among its defeated neighbours, so that was a given too. At some point, however, if the transplant is to take, the new country has to move on from wars and start making deals that cement its place in the region. That is bound to be tricky because of all the resentment that the wars have generated, but by the early 1990s Israel had reached that point, at least in the view of some of its leaders. What nobody had taken sufficiently into account was the psychological impact of all these defeats on the populations of the Arab countries.

Roll back the tape to the 1940s and 1950s. Arab states newly emerged from colonial rule are looking for some quick way to escape their backwardness and poverty. Overwhelmingly the larger countries – Egypt, Algeria, Syria, Iraq – opt for secular socialist regimes, mostly led by military men, which they hope will enable them to catch up with their former European oppressors as fast as the Soviet Union is catching up (or seems to be catching up) with its Western rivals. A generation of young Arab revolutionaries, most of whom rarely see the inside of a mosque, promise to build countries that can both make their people prosperous and take on Israel as an equal.

They believe what they say, but it's nonsense: the system they have adopted isn't really even working very well in Eastern Europe, and in the Middle East they are starting from a lot farther back in terms of industrial plant, scientific resources, and educated people.

The overwhelming Israeli military victory of 1967 and the accompanying fourfold expansion of Israeli territory, accomplished without any British or French help, was a blow to the reputation of the secular "socialist" regimes of the Arab world from which they never recovered. They hadn't delivered the goods economically, and they couldn't beat Israel either. But the strange and crippling thing is that they didn't disappear beneath a wave of righteous public anger. They are all still there, almost forty years after their sell-by date, no longer really socialist but still very much in power: the Armée de libération nationale (ALN) generals in Algeria, so secretive that they don't even like their names to be known to the public; Hosni Mubarak in Egypt, third in a series of military officers who have monopolized power in Egypt for a full fifty years; the Assad clan in Syria, now in its second generation of presidents – and until very recently, Saddam Hussein and the Baath Party in Iraq.

What saved the military/socialist secular regimes of the Arab world was the Cold War. The Soviet Union had been an early supporter of Israel, racing with the United States to be the first to recognize its independence because it reckoned that the dominant socialist tradition within the Zionist movement would make the new state a natural ally. The United States, quite wisely, refused to be drawn into the Arab-Israeli military confrontation on either side; most Americans undoubtedly wished Israel well, but practical US interests in the region were mostly in the oil-rich parts of the Arab world. Indeed, during the 1950s and the early 1960s Israel's principal military supplier was not the United States but France (which is even alleged to have helped Israel to develop its nuclear weapons).

At the end of the 1950s, however, Israel's Arab opponents,

finding no Western country willing to sell them the arms they needed to fight Israel on equal terms, turned to the Soviet Union. Moscow was receptive, having by now abandoned its earlier hope that Israel could be a reliable Middle Eastern base and ally, so it happily sold arms to Egypt, Syria, and Iraq – and suddenly the Cold War arrived in the Middle East. The United States took over as Israel's main arms supplier, and in return Israel became America's principal Middle Eastern ally and base.

The utter defeat and humiliation of the Arab states in the 1967 war should have destroyed the old military/socialist regimes, but they survived because by then the Soviet Union was functioning as a sort of external life-support system. As the Soviet Union's economic difficulties grew and it got less generous, the Egyptian regime switched to American life-support in the mid-1970s. (Egypt is now the second-largest recipient of American foreign aid – after Israel.) Saddam Hussein's Baathist regime in Iraq also switched its primary foreign alliance from the Soviet Union to the United States in the 1980s (because Saddam was then fighting Iran, an American enemy). Eventually, after the 1991 elections in Algeria had to be cancelled by the regime to prevent Islamists from winning, even the Algerian generals signed on. None of these Arab regimes was troubled by the fact that the United States was also Israel's principal military supplier and diplomatic supporter, for by then not even Egypt worried about having to fight Israel again. Indeed, Egypt formally made peace with Israel in 1979.

By the late 1970s it was recognized by all serious military observers that Israel's Arab neighbours could not attack it again with any hope of success. Israel's armed forces were by far the strongest in the region; it had an absolute monopoly of nuclear weapons and long-range delivery systems and could destroy any Arab city at short notice without fear of retaliation; and the United States backed it 110 per cent. No Arab attack could possibly succeed – and by the early

1980s Arab regimes had stopped buying weapons of the types and in the quantities that would even put them in the same military league as the Israelis. A perfectly rational decision – but how did ordinary Arabs feel about it?

Terrible, of course, and deeply betrayed. Their dictators had promised development and promised victory over Israel. They had delivered on neither – but they were still there, comfortable in their palaces, and now they had given up even thinking about taking Israel on. It was in this post-1967 atmosphere of defeat and perceived betrayal that Arabs first turned to Islamist explanations of what was wrong and Islamist programmes for fixing it.

The word *Islamist* is better than *fundamentalist* because Islamism is a political project based on a religious interpretation of what is happening in the world, whereas fundamentalism ... well, actually, fundamentalism is a Christian concept, and in Islam it is virtually meaningless. The two religions draw so heavily on Judaism in their vision of God and their moral categories that they have sometimes been described as twin Jewish heresies, but in the matter of scripture there is a huge difference between them – and fundamentalism is all about scripture.

Both the old and the new testaments of the Bible were written by a number of different individuals, and the various prophets and evangelists don't always agree on the details. So Christians are free to believe the gospel of Luke, for example, which claims that a Roman census obliged Jesus's father, Joseph, to return to his birthplace to be counted, thus ensuring that Jesus was born at Bethlehem in Judaea. Or they can observe that none of the other gospels mentions this story, that there is no other record of this alleged census, that the ultra-practical Romans were not likely to do something as pointless and crazy as insisting that everybody return to their birthplace to be counted – but that Luke's story conveniently deals with the awkward fact that Jesus grew up in Galilee, whereas prophecy stated clearly that the Messiah would be born in Judaea. The very nature of Christian scripture encourages a diversity of interpretations, and so there is a special name for those who accept every word of the Bible literally (ignoring the numerous contradictions): fundamentalists.

The Quran is different, because it was not written by a number of men. In fact, Muslims believe that it was not written by a man at all: rather, it is the direct word of God as dictated to and written down by the prophet Muhammad. Because it has only one author, it is a far more unified text, containing no glaring contradictions of fact – and *all* Muslims are fundamentalists in the sense that they are bound to accept the Quran as literally the words of God. That does not mean that all Muslims are rigidly conservative in the way they interpret God's will in their daily lives; every religious community finds ways to contain and express the diversity of human personality and experience, and Islam does it as well as any. There are liberal Muslims, there are conservative Muslims, and there are some very radical Muslims indeed, but *fundamentalism* in the Christian sense has no meaning in Islam.

The reason that so many Western observers have given this label to radical Muslims is that, like Christian fundamentalists, they are both socially conservative and politically engaged. Both movements are in revolt against the increasing secularization of their societies, which they experience as destructive. They see themselves as last-ditch defenders of key values that are under attack – from the "liberal establishment" at home, in the case of Western fundamentalists, but also from the foreign and aggressive culture of the West, in the eyes of Islamist radicals. However violent and apparently aggressive their actions, they see themselves as acting defensively:

most Islamists believe quite literally that the entire Muslim world is under attack by a "Crusader–Zionist conspiracy" that intends to destroy it. Most US actions since 9/11, particularly the invasion of Iraq, are seen by Islamists as evidence that this is true – and this interpretation is gaining ground in the broader Muslim community as well.

The fact that the Islamists have turned themselves into a revolutionary political movement is not intrinsically wrong or sinful in Muslim eyes, because religious movements have often played that role in Muslim history. From its earliest days, Islam was the religion of conquerors and of the state itself, so it does not make the same distinction between sacred and secular power as Christianity, which spent its formative years as the religion of underdogs, outsiders, and slaves. Indeed, since the authority of the Muslim ruler came from God, anybody wanting to oppose or overthrow an existing Muslim government had to couch his criticisms in religious language, accusing the ruler of failing to respect and uphold true Islamic principles.

In politics, as in ecology, every niche is filled. From the beginning of the eighteenth century, Muslim governments that were scrambling to respond to the overwhelming challenge from the West by adopting Western technology and organization invariably faced domestic opponents who criticized them for neglecting Islamic traditions and values. Some of the critics were genuinely appalled at the idea that the perfect ordering of Islamic society ordained by God (in their understanding of His word) should be changed simply to counter the threat from the European empires; others had more personal motives for their opposition, but found the religious critique a useful stick to beat the regime with. And some of the reformist rulers – especially in the Ottoman Empire – did get overthrown and killed.

As the railways, telegraph lines, and steamship routes of the nine-

teenth-century European empires brought the far-flung parts of the
Muslim world more directly into contact than ever before, something else began to take shape: a political concept that you could call
Islamist, though the preferred term at the time was *pan-Islamic*. The
chief purveyors of this idea were the rulers of the last surviving
Muslim empire, the Turks, and their vehicle was the caliphate, once
the centre of political and religious authority in the early Islamic
empire. The Turks had unilaterally moved the seat of the more or
less defunct caliphate from Cairo to Istanbul in the sixteenth
century when they conquered Egypt, and the Ottoman sultans had
appropriated the title of caliph for themselves, but at that time it
meant little. Even in the glory days of the eighth and ninth centuries
the caliphate governed fewer than half of the world's Muslims, and
it had long since lost all real authority. But in the last days of
Ottoman decline, after the radical officers known as the Young
Turks seized power in 1908 in a desperate attempt to save the
empire, pan-Islamism became a central part of their strategy.

The idea was to turn the moribund caliphate into a meaningful
symbol of Muslim unity. The sultan (and caliph) was now a mere
puppet in the hands of the Young Turk officers, many of whom were
not religious at all, but if he could serve as a focus of Muslim loyalty
that rose above language and ethnicity and bound Arabs and Kurds
to the Turkish-run empire, that would be quite useful. If he could
also embody the spirit of Islamic unity and resistance to European
conquest for the hundreds of millions of Muslims living under
European rule, and perhaps inspire them to revolt against their
Christian imperial masters, even better.

The pan-Islamic propaganda machine ran full blast for ten years,
until the final collapse of the Ottoman Empire in 1918 – but nobody
paid any attention. When the First World War broke out in 1914,
Indian Muslims fought willingly for the British Empire against the
Turks, North African Muslims served France on the Western Front,

Central Asian Muslims failed to revolt against their Russian rulers – and the Arabs did revolt against the Turks. The whole pan-Islamic idea failed so dramatically and comprehensively that it did not resurface in public again for fifty years.

It was Mustafa Kemal Atatürk, a member of the original Young Turk revolutionary group, who hammered the message home. He had consistently argued to his Young Turk colleagues that the pan-Islamic approach was doomed and that the only hope was to salvage a Turkish national state from the wreckage of the empire, and he proved to be spectacularly right. Turkey had lost the war and the empire by 1918, but Atatürk created a resistance movement and eventually an army that defeated the attempt of the victorious Entente powers to divide Turkey up among themselves. Once the Turkish republic was safe, he contemptuously abolished the caliphate in 1923.

Atatürk was a profoundly secular man, and his strategy for modernization was broadly followed by practically every other Muslim country that gained its freedom in the next half-century, though not always with the same success that he had in the Turkish republic. The formula was nationalism, a strong, secular state, and the wholesale adoption of Western models in every domain of public life from government and industry to education and civil law. Give or take a bit, Sukarno and Suharto followed the same course in Indonesia, as did Muhammad Ali Jinnah, Zulfikar Ali Bhutto, and Muhammad Ayub Khan in Pakistan, the Shah in Iran, the Baath Party in Iraq and Syria, Gamal Abdel Nasser and his successors in Egypt, and the Front de Libération Nationale (FLN) in Algeria. In some places, it worked reasonably well. In the Arab world, it didn't.

After the stunning and completely unforeseen Arab defeat at the hands of Israel in 1967, Arab nationalism was deeply wounded and the pan-Arab movement was stone dead. The secular, socialist path to modernization was discredited, and a generation of desperate young Arabs was ready to listen to almost any other solution that sounded plausible. The Islamists filled the vacuum.

There had always been radical Muslim groups around who condemned the existing governments as insufficiently Islamic; it was a normal part of politics in Muslim countries. Their numbers grew and their critique sharpened as the secular Arab governments demonstrated their total inability to deal with the problems they confronted, and by the early 1970s they had achieved critical mass in a number of Arab countries: they became actual revolutionary movements. Their analysis of the problem was crude, but it had an undeniable appeal because of its very simplicity.

They began with a question. Why, after a thousand years of brilliant success in every field – political, military, scientific, commercial, and cultural – have Muslims been losing on every front for the past several hundred years? We Muslims presumably owed our successes to God's favour, for we are His people, so we must conclude that His favour has now been withdrawn. Therefore the key question is: What are we doing that has caused God to turn away from us?

As with all such rhetorical questions, the answer is only a split second away. It is that ever since we Muslims were first confronted with the challenge of the West a few hundred years ago, our dominant strategy for coping with the threat has been to *copy* the West. We have not only copied Western technology, but we have also adopted Western ideas, perspectives, institutions, and behaviours. In doing so, we have abandoned our own Islamic traditions and values – so God has ceased to help us.

It is a perfectly rational argument, if you accept the initial premise that all the successes or failures of Muslims in the world are directly dependent on God's favour (which is a premise that many Muslims are willing to accept). It is also a very attractive argument to people who are close to despair, because it says that the solution lies in your own hands. The problem is not that the Arab world is several generations behind the West in its technological skills, its industrial strength, its educational level, and its political and social ability to compete in a globalized world (which is a deeply depressing answer, since it means that it will take several generations to fix). Rather, the problem is simply that Muslims are living the wrong way – and that's easy to fix. All we have to do is start living the way God truly wants Muslims to live, and then He will be at our side again and we will start to win.

It is not a new argument. In fact, it has been deployed against many Muslim regimes for many centuries past. A Muslim ruler who crossed some powerful vested interest or had the bad luck to preside over a military or economic disaster could always count on some group of bearded fanatics with a political agenda proclaiming that he had strayed from the path of righteousness and no longer deserved to rule over good Muslims. It was the only morally correct solution to the problem of how to remove a Muslim ruler who theoretically governed with God's authority, the Islamic equivalent of the Chinese device of declaring that a divine emperor had "lost the Mandate of Heaven."

Of course, there was plainly something anachronistic about resurrecting this old argument and strategy in the latter half of the twentieth century, for use against secular, so-called socialist regimes that did not even bother to claim Islamic legitimacy for their rule. On the other hand, it could be a good way to mobilize people for yet one more try at breaking the stagnation and defeatism that paralyzed the Arab world, and what other arguments and strategies were left? As British diplomat James Craig reported back to the Foreign Office after a tour of several Arab countries in 1972, when Arab morale was at the very nadir: "One theory put to me was that, since Arab nationalism had manifestly failed, people are turning to the alternative of Islamic nationalism. I argued that this, too, had failed

– indeed, it failed long ago. The reply was that the very length of time which had passed since this failure made it possible to consider giving it a second trial run."

You will have noticed how this discussion lurches back and forth between talking specifically about Arabs and more generally about Muslims. It does so because that is precisely what the arguments of both the Arab nationalists and the devout Islamists were doing in the late 1960s and early 1970s, as the old certainties of the secular modernizers lost credibility.

Theologically, the Islamist position is profoundly anti-nationalist. It comes out of the Salafist tradition, an intensely romantic vision in which the world's 1.3 billion Muslims, living in forty-odd countries spread across three continents, return to the ideals of the first generations of Muslims and live as one under Sharia law in a single, borderless community. Nation-states based on shared language and history are idolatry and blasphemy and only distract the attention of Muslims from the one community they really owe loyalty to: the *umma*, the worldwide community of all Muslim believers. As Osama bin Laden put it in a tape broadcast in February 2003, just before the US invasion of Iraq: "The fighting should be in the name of God only, not in the name of national ideologies, nor to seek victory for the ignorant governments that rule all Arab states, including Iraq."

The paradox is that while Islamism is an anti-national doctrine, most of the Muslims who have been attracted to it are Arab nationalists – because Arabs are the only large Muslim group whose situation is so desperate that many of them have been tempted to turn to such a radical doctrine. Some people try to force Iran into the same category, but the "Islamic revolution" in Iran in 1978–79 was in no sense an Islamist phenomenon. It was another example of conservative Muslim revolt against a radical project for Westernization by a secular modernizer, Shah Reza Pahlavi, but it completely lacked the apocalyptic world-changing ambitions of the Islamists. As Shias, Iranians belong to a minority sect of Islam that is seen as verging on the heretical by Sunnis, who account for perhaps 90 per cent of Muslims worldwide. Shias could not rationally share the goal of a single borderless Muslim world-state run by Sunni Islamist fanatics, whose first act would be to crush dissenters like themselves. The Iranian Revolution was just about Iran, and although the Iranian mullahs run a thoroughly oppressive theocracy, by no stretch of the imagination could they be called Islamists in the current measure of that word.

Arabs are certainly not the only Muslim group that has been attracted to the radical doctrines of the Islamists. There is more support for Islamism among Pakistanis than in any other large non-Arab group because of the radicalizing effects of the long confrontation with India, and latterly there has been considerable radicalization among some small Muslim groups who have come under extreme pressure: Chechens and Bosnian Muslims, for example, although they used to be among the most secular Muslims on the planet. But it remains true that the great majority of the committed Islamists in the world are Arabs, although less than a quarter of the world's Muslims are Arabs. Support for Islamist ideals (if not always for Islamist tactics) probably ranges between 10 and 15 per cent of the population in most Arab countries, though there are no reliable opinion polls on this subject.

The grievances of Arab Islamists are overwhelmingly about the plight of the Arab world, though in recent years they have tactfully added the plight of Chechens, Moros in the southern Philippines, and other small, beleaguered Muslim communities to their list. They reconcile their very Arab-centred priorities with their pan-Islamic ideology by arguing that there is a worldwide conspiracy of Christians and Jews to destroy Islam – the "Crusader–Zionist plot" – and that the plotters have chosen the Arab countries, the very heart of the Muslim world, as the primary target for their attacks. In defending Arab interests, they argue, they are effectively defending all of Islam, and one day their struggle will have the active support of all 1.3 billion Muslims. But you have to start from where you are, so in practice they began their active operations among the 300 million people of the Arab world.

Islamism is not just an ideology; it is a political programme for changing the world so that Muslims are no longer victims. Having defined the phenomenon of continuous Muslim defeats during the past few centuries as a moral rather than a practical problem, the Islamists devised a two-stage project for turning history around. The first priority is to get God back on the side of the Muslims, which means forcing the masses to abandon their corrupt, half-Westernized ways and get back to the way of life that God really demands of good Muslims (in the extreme and rigid form that the Islamists view as God's will). This means in practice that the Islamists must seize control of the state and use its power to *force* Muslims back into the right ways. Islamists are of necessity revolutionaries, and the first stage of their project requires the overthrow of the existing government in every Muslim country and its replacement by (of course) themselves.

Having accomplished this not unambitious goal and reformed all the societies of the Muslim world to conform to God's true requirements, they would then move on to the second stage of the project: the unification of the entire Muslim population of the planet in a single transnational super-state. Then, with God on their side, the united Muslims of the world will take on the West's hated domination of the planet and destroy it.

The Islamists are a classic example of a group of people who are dangerous but not really serious. Their analysis is quite rational if you share their frame of reference (though the great majority of Muslims do not accept it). Bits of their programme could work, like seizing power in one or more Arab countries, because there are a lot of very unhappy people in those countries, and Western overreaction to the Islamist terrorists is making them more unhappy. But taking power everywhere, uniting the whole Muslim world in a single super-state, and launching the final jihad against the infidels – that is dreaming in Technicolor. If you doubt that, consider Afghanistan.

In 1996 a group of Islamists called the Taliban (literally, "students of religion") came to power in Afghanistan. Ten years of Soviet occupation and guerrilla resistance, followed by seven years of civil war, had almost destroyed the country, and most Afghans were ready to accept any government that could stop the fighting. Even so, the Taliban would never have won without the strong support of Pakistan's Inter-Service Intelligence (ISI) agency, which saw them as a means of controlling a turbulent neighbour. But what happened once the Taliban were actually in power is very instructive, for they did none of the things that normal governments do.

They paid virtually no attention to public health or education (apart from having girls expelled from school), or even to trade and commerce. Instead, they put most of their energy into obsessing about the smallest details of the public's dress and behaviour. Men were punished for not growing their beards (un-Islamic) or for secretly trimming them (also un-Islamic); women were whipped for appearing in public without the company of a male relative, or with a square inch of skin showing somewhere; music was banned, video-tapes were ceremoniously hanged, every pettiness imaginable was indulged.

Arab Islamists are doubtless somewhat more sophisticated than their Afghan country cousins, but they do inhabit the same territory. Indeed, many of the younger Arab leaders of the Islamist movement were resident in Afghanistan throughout the Taliban period, and gave no sign that they disapproved of the Taliban's behaviour. What seem like mere distractions and diversions of effort to outsiders are actually the heart of the matter to Islamists: it is only by getting the details of dress and behaviour exactly right that Muslims will once more be living in a way that pleases God, and therefore once again enjoy his support. The trivial stuff *is* the important stuff: get that right and God will take care of the rest.

The fact that the Islamists really would behave like this if they ever got power elsewhere, which is now widely understood, imposes a ceiling of sorts on their potential support. That kind of society has strong appeal among the dispossessed and desperate because of its intense egalitarianism, and it appeals also to conservative men of any class who feel threatened by the social changes – especially changes in the status of women and the deference of the young for the old – that are underway in the Muslim world. (Christian fundamentalists, of course, are largely drawn from precisely the same groups.) These social groups would not normally comprise a majority in any Muslim society, however, and the images and stories coming out of Afghanistan under Taliban rule were profoundly distasteful and disturbing to most Muslims elsewhere. That doesn't mean that the Islamists can never win anywhere: one can imagine some cataclysmic revolution bringing hard-line Islamists to power even in a relatively modern and sophisticated country like Algeria or Iraq. After all, something rather similar happened in Iran twenty-five years ago. But it isn't going to happen all over the place. Muslims aren't stupid, and the vast majority of them don't want to live like that. Moreover, the better-educated among them are well aware of how un-Islamic the Islamists are.

The Islamists have grafted the Western concept of the nation-state (founded in this case on shared religion, not common language or ethnicity) onto the traditional Islamic idea of the *umma*, which is a community of believers, not a state. Worse, they have borrowed the distinctively Western idea of transforming the world through terror

– as practised by Jacobins, anarchists, Bolsheviks, and many lesser groups of fanatics down to Sendero Luminoso and the Baader–Meinhof Gang – in order to create a utopia. In the case of the Islamists, that utopia may have a rather medieval look to it, but they are thoroughly modern men with a huge Western component in their thinking. Osama bin Laden grew up in jeans, not robes.

"[Osama bin Laden's] utopian vision of the future – a harmonious world in which the traditional institutions of government are no longer necessary – is an echo of nineteenth-century European anarchism. Like the anarchists, bin Laden believes corrupt power structures can be destroyed by acts of spectacular violence ... When he calls on his followers to remake the world through terror, he speaks in a modern Western voice ... With its radical utopianism and boundless faith in the human will, al Qaeda belongs in our world, not the medieval past."

– John Grey, *Al Qaeda and What It Means To Be Modern* (2004)

All of the early Islamist attacks were in the Arab world, because that was where the Islamists themselves came from. Every existing Arab regime was their enemy, and they made no distinction between secular republics like Egypt and traditional monarchies like Saudi Arabia – nor, indeed, between pro-American regimes like both of the above and pro-Soviet ones like Syria. In the eyes of the Islamists all the existing regimes were equally corrupt. Their first attack was a commando-style assault on the Grand Mosque in Mecca itself, Islam's most sacred site, by several hundred armed men in 1979. They held it for more than two weeks before being overwhelmed in heavy fighting; the survivors were executed by the Saudi regime.

A common feature of all these early operations, like the assassination of Egyptian president Anwar Sadat in 1981 or the large-scale uprising by the Muslim Brotherhood in the Syrian city of Hama in 1982, was that the planners naively shared the old anarchists' faith in the transformative power of violence: they genuinely expected masses of people to flock to the Islamists' banner once they gave the signal with their attack. It didn't happen. There had been a drift back to the mosques in the Arab world in the last three decades of the twentieth century, in reaction to the perceived failure of the project for high-speed modernization on the Western model, but it didn't mean that large numbers of ordinary Arab men and women were willing to risk their lives to help bring the Islamists to power. And if they weren't willing to do that, then the Islamists could not win power.

If you are seeking to overthrow a government from below, there are only two ways that work. One is to find allies in the armed forces and have them do it for you through a military coup. This route was closed off to the Islamists from the start, because the officer corps of Arab armies were the stronghold of the secular modernizers – and ever since the military recognized the Islamist threat, they have been very careful to weed out young officers at the first sign of Islamist sympathies. The other way to overthrow a government is in the streets, either by violent revolution or even, in some recent cases, non-violently, but either of these tactics requires a very large number of people to get out in the streets and challenge the existing regime – and for the Arab Islamists, people were simply not willing to take that risk. Most Arabs do not love the governments they live under, but they do not love or trust the Islamists either. They stayed at home in droves when the Islamists raised the banner of revolt, and stage one of the Islamist project ran straight onto the rocks.

By the mid-1980s, stalemate had set in throughout the Arab world. The Islamist revolutionaries were still there in every major Arab country, carrying out occasional terrorist attacks, but they were making no noticeable headway politically. The general view was that they were a violent nuisance but essentially a spent force: when the Palestinian Islamist group Hamas was founded in 1987, the Israeli secret service at first encouraged and subsidized it as a useful counter-weight to Yasser Arafat's secular Palestine Liberation Organization, which was seen as a far more dangerous opponent. But there was one place where Islamists actually were making a difference: not an Arab country at all, but Afghanistan. And it was there that a new generation of Islamists learned to move beyond mere exemplary violence and discovered strategy.

The Soviet invasion of Afghanistan in 1979 was an apparent triumph of American foreign policy, which had been seeking for years to turn Afghanistan into "Russia's Vietnam." Under the Carter administration in the later 1970s, National Security Adviser Zbigniew Brzezinski authorized a secret flow of arms and money to the Afghan tribes to encourage them to rise in revolt against the modernizing, secular, and pro-Soviet regime in Kabul. It was a strategy that allied America not only with the most deeply conservative Muslim forces in Afghanistan but also with the most radical Islamists in the Arab world, and nobody in Washington minded. Like Anwar Sadat in Egypt in the 1970s, who initially courted the Islamists as a potential source of support and was eventually assassinated by them, or the Israelis in the late 1980s helping to set up Hamas in the occupied territories, the United States was confident that it could exploit and control the Islamists for its own purposes.

Washington's ultimate goal in backing the Afghan insurgents was to force Moscow to intervene militarily to save the Kabul regime. Then, once the Soviet Union had been lured into invading, the United States would ally itself with local and foreign Islamist forces to get a full-scale revolt going against the Soviet occupation. After all, as Brzezinski remarked long afterwards, in 1998: "What is most important in the history of the world? The Taliban or the collapse of the Soviet Empire? Some stirred-up Muslims or the liberation of Central Europe and the end of the Cold War?"

Brzezinski really believes that the ten-year Russian debacle in

Afghanistan was the cause of the old Soviet Union's final collapse in 1991. The rest of us are free to doubt it, but the United States certainly did inflict a long ordeal on the Russians, who lost fifteen thousand soldiers killed before they finally withdrew from Afghanistan in 1989. The Afghan people paid a far higher price, including hundreds of thousands killed and millions made refugees. But Americans paid a price in the end too, because Afghanistan is where the new Islamist strategy that ultimately led to 9/11 gradually came into focus.

Young Islamists from all over the Arab world flocked to Afghanistan to fight against the infidel Russian invaders: it was simultaneously an opportunity to serve Islam and a way to escape from the demoralizing stalemate at home. (Many volunteers also came from Pakistan and a few from other Muslim countries, but most of the foreign Islamists in Afghanistan were Arabs.) Much of their money and most of their weapons came directly or indirectly from the Central Intelligence Agency, the Defense Intelligence Agency, and other covert organizations working for the US government, which is why it is sometimes said that the United States "created" Osama bin Laden and al-Qaeda. It would be more accurate to say that it successfully used the Islamists to attain its goals – and inadvertently created a monster in the process.

It seems unlikely that the scattered Islamist movements of the various Muslim countries, each largely trapped behind its own frontiers, could ever have achieved even the limited degree of coordination they now have if thousands of their members had not spent years waging a jihad together in the crucible of Afghanistan. It is even less likely that they would have arrived at the new strategy of attacking the West directly without the experience of that war fought so far from home. In any case, it is clear that the first foundations of what we know as al-Qaeda (an abstract noun meaning "network" or "base") were laid in Afghanistan in 1989, in the triumphant aftermath of the Soviet withdrawal, by Osama bin Laden and other "Arab Afghan" veterans of the anti-Soviet jihad. Al-Qaeda was only one among many similar Islamist organizations, united in basic ideology and ultimate goals but divided by personalities and methods, that were springing up, merging, and dissolving amid the wreckage of post–Soviet Afghanistan, but bin Laden had charisma, money (he came from a very rich Saudi family), and real organizing ability, so his outfit grew fast.

From the beginning, one thing in particular distinguished al-Qaeda and its many rivals in Afghanistan from the existing Islamist movements in the various Arab countries. All of the latter aimed to overthrow the secular governments of the Muslim world, stage one in the Islamist project, by direct attacks against those governments. The Arab mujahedeen in Afghanistan believed that this approach simply wasn't working. Terrorist attacks inside the Muslim countries had propaganda value in getting the Islamists' programme before the public, but they did not win enough support to get the Arab masses out in the streets in support of the Islamist cause, so the revolutions remained forever stalled. It was in Afghanistan that the "Arab Afghans" came up with the idea of attacking the West directly by terrorist means.

This idea may initially have been just an attractive option for men who had learned to think and act transnationally, and were ready to move on from attacking Russians to attacking Americans. Just a little further thought, however, would have revealed to them that such attacks could yield more than propaganda success. If their attacks could draw the Americans and other Westerners into striking back militarily against the Muslim world from which the terrorism was coming, then those counter-strikes might finally drive the masses into the arms of the Islamists, and they could at last get their long-stalled revolutions off the ground. It was a roundabout route to their goal, to be sure, but sometimes the longest way round is the shortest way home.

This was hardly an original insight. Almost all terrorism is a form of political jiu-jitsu in which the weaker side (the terrorists) tries to trick the stronger side (the government, the colonial power, etc.) into an overreaction that really serves the terrorists' goals. When military staff colleges teach the theory of guerrilla war and terrorism to Western officers, the point they always stress is that the guerrillas or terrorists are never trying to win a victory on the battlefield. They can't; they don't have enough force. Instead, they are using the very limited amount of force at their disposal in ways that will goad you, the army, into using your overwhelming force in ways that help their cause and hurt yours.

The struggle will be decided, in the end, not by who wins the battles but by which way the mass of the population jumps, into their camp or into yours – and it is all too easy to trick an army into using the huge amounts of power at its disposal in ways that will fatally alienate a population. The US army won almost every battle in Vietnam but lost the war. The same was true of the British in Kenya, Cyprus, and Aden, of the French in Vietnam and Algeria, of the Portuguese in Angola and Mozambique, of the Russians in Afghanistan – the list goes on.

Some will object that those were guerrilla wars, "people's wars," whereas pure terrorism conducted by small groups of ruthless ideologues has a much less impressive record: where are the Montoneros and the Red Brigades, the Weathermen and the Symbionese Liberation Army today? But big and successful guerrilla armies like the Vietcong, the FLN in Algeria, and Frelimo in Mozambique all started out as small groups of ruthless ideologues employing purely terrorist means. They just managed to attract enough popular support to grow into larger organizations capable of full-scale military operations in the later stages of their liberation wars. The real distinction is not between terrorists (ideologues using force for evil ends) and guerrillas (nationalists using force for more or less good ends). It is between revolutionaries who are using terror against their own people, and those who are using it against foreigners. The former almost never succeed; the latter usually do – so if you're stuck in the former group (as the Islamists of the Arab world still were in 1990), you would be wise to move yourself into the latter group.

Compare the Islamist revolutionaries who emerged in Algeria in the early 1990s with the original Algerian revolutionaries and freedom-fighters of the 1950s. They both had ideologies that were not shared by the majority of the population (Islamist in the latter case, Marxist in the former), and their goal in both cases was to turn the population against the existing government and take its place. The difference was that the FLN in Algeria in the 1950s had the French army and a million French settlers to attack. It used terrorism against collaborators among the Muslim population of Algeria too, but the reason for its eventual success was that its terrorist attacks against French civilians in Algeria and in France itself tricked the French army into savage repression and indiscriminate reprisals. The Muslim population was eventually driven into the FLN's arms, and although the French army was never defeated in the field it eventually gave up and went home, abandoning its local allies to their fate.

Contrast the fate of the Groupes Islamiques Armées (GIA) and the other Islamist fighting groups that proliferated in Algeria after the shadowy group of generals who rule the country cancelled the 1991 elections when it became clear that Islamic parties would win in the second round. The rebels began with a much broader base of support than the FLN did thirty-five years earlier – many Algerians had turned to conservative forms of Islam in reaction to decades of repression and growing poverty, though few were explicitly Islamist – and yet they are now virtually extinct. Their problem was that there were no targets available who weren't Algerian. The GIA began by trying to kill regime members, but since those targets were generally too well protected, they ended up mostly killing villagers who co-operated (often under duress) with the regime.

This was so counterproductive in terms of the struggle for public opinion that eventually the Algerian army started mimicking the terrorists' behaviour in order to reinforce the effect: it would send out soldiers disguised as terrorists to massacre yet more villagers who were co-operating with the government. In ten years, about a hundred and twenty thousand people were murdered, usually in ghastly ways, but you don't win people's hearts and minds by killing their relatives and friends: the Islamist terrorists in Algeria never built mass support and are now a spent force. How different it would have been if Algeria had still been occupied by foreign troops, and the GIA could have built its strategy, FLN-style, around getting those foreign troops to commit atrocities against ordinary Algerians.

The dilemma of the whole Islamist revolutionary movement in the Arab world in the 1990s was the GIA's dilemma writ large: their project was stalled at the first stage because their countries were formally independent, and there was nobody around to kill except Arabs. Assassinating leading figures in the local regimes was an unrewarding business, because governments are enormous bureaucracies that can easily fill the vacancies you create – and being local regimes, they were rarely stupid enough to commit indiscriminate massacres that would drive local people into the arms of the Islamists. Going the GIA route and directly trying to terrorize your own people into supporting you won't work either. What you need here is to get some foreigners involved.

The new Islamist strategy that emerged in the camps of the "Arab Afghans" at the end of the war in Afghanistan put the highest priority on attacks against Westerners, and above all Americans.

Whenever possible, these attacks should be in Western countries. The aim was to lure Western governments into indiscriminate counter-attacks against Muslim countries, and ideally even invasions that put Western troops on the ground in the Muslim world. The ultimate purpose was to recreate the conditions of a classic liberation war, where every bullet the foreign troops fire creates another recruit to the cause, and ultimately the Islamists win and the Americans go home because the Islamists are local patriots and Americans are foreigners. Then, once the rebels are in power, they impose their Islamist ideology, force everybody into the right ways of believing and behaving, and move on to the second stage of the grand project for putting Muslims back on top.

The founders of al-Qaeda were sitting in Afghanistan at the end of a ten-year war in which the United States had lured the Soviet Union into invading a Muslim country; the Soviet army had been chewed to bits in the subsequent war; and the Afghan people had been so radicalized by the invasion that the local Islamists, the Taliban, would soon come to power there. What could be more obvious than to think about tricking the United States into blundering into the same trap? So they set about building an organization to do just that.

I meet some resistance from Western audiences every time I discuss this Islamist strategy in public, and there are three main objections. One: Terrorists are just evil, and we shouldn't concern ourselves with their motives and methods. Two: Islamists are ignorant fanatics with a medieval worldview, so they are incapable of such a sophisticated strategy. Three: There is nothing in their writings and statements that refers to this strategy.

So, then, one: Being wicked doesn't make people stupid, any more than being good makes them bright. If you don't understand the terrorists' motives and methods, they will run circles around you.

Two: Islamists are indeed fanatics, but they are thoroughly

modern fanatics with laptops, well-used passports, and long lines of credit. The leading cadres are intelligent men who are fully familiar with modern theories and ideas: some of them will probably read this book, as they read everything that pertains to their trade and mission. They would be derelict in their duty if they did not understand the history and theory of their chosen technique, terrorism.

And three: They would be equally derelict if they ever discussed their strategy in public. They talk freely about their motives and their goals, but they obviously should never openly discuss a strategy that aims to recruit people to their cause by tricking powerful strangers into inflicting death and destruction on them.

The initial idea of a terrorist organization that specifically targeted the West was hatched in Afghanistan in 1989–90, but it took some time to build it because the recently liberated country soon tumbled into a destructive civil war between the ethnically divided local mujahedeen groups who had united only to fight the Russians. Osama bin Laden arrived home in Saudi Arabia in 1990, just in time to witness the panic in Riyadh when the Iraqi army invaded the neighbouring mini-state of Kuwait. (The Saudi media were not allowed to report the invasion for one hundred hours.) The story goes that he offered the services of his "Arab Afghans" to defend Saudi Arabia from Saddam Hussein's tanks, which may be true: he despised the cynical combination of religious conservatism and grotesque corruption that characterized the Saudi ruling family, but he loathed the outright secularism of Saddam Hussein's regime even more. At any rate, the Saudi regime did not accept his services, opting instead to invite American troops into the kingdom – and at that point, bin Laden crossed the line and became an outlaw.

His open vilification of the Saudi regime for allowing infidel soldiers into the "land of the two holy cities" (Mecca and Medina) led to his expulsion from Arabia, and later to the cancellation of his citizenship. He took up residence in Sudan for some years, sustained by his own ample resources of cash and a growing flow of money from Islamists in Western countries. While he was in Sudan his network of contacts and collaborators grew rapidly, and his particular interest in Muslims living in the West became evident. In 1996, after the Taliban gained power in Kabul, he moved the operation back to Afghanistan and set up training camps in which the principles and techniques of terrorism were taught.

During the later 1990s, somewhere between 20,000 and 70,000 people from about fifty countries passed through al-Qaeda's training camps in Afghanistan – "a terrorist Disneyland where you could meet anyone from any Islamist group," in the words of Rohan Gunaratna of the Institute of Defence and Strategic Studies in Singapore – and through other camps that were open for shorter periods in Yemen and Sudan. Al-Qaeda members, almost all drawn from the old "Arab Afghans" who had fought the Soviets, taught them secure communications techniques, the use of explosives, all the usual terrorist lore, and then the graduates returned home – but most of them had no further direct contact with al-Qaeda. Having honed their ideology and their "craft," they were sent on their way to make up their own role in the struggle. Some would subsequently found their own Islamist organizations, or had already done so before arriving in Afghanistan; al-Qaeda's leaders didn't mind. It is wrong even to think of al-Qaeda as a franchise operation, though that is getting closer: one witness at the trial after the bombings of US embassies in East Africa in 1998 referred to it as a "formula system" for terrorism, a formula that could be exported and adapted to any environment.

The truth is that al-Qaeda hardly even exists – at least, not in the sense that formal bureaucratic organizations like Shell Oil or the US Marine Corps exist. Terrorist groups have always been highly decentralized and divided into a cellular structure to minimize the damage when security forces penetrate their organization, but al-

Qaeda went further than that. Even at the time of its creation, it had no formal boundary that separated members from non-members. There was a geographically dispersed inner group of ideologues and planners, probably numbering only in the hundreds, who served as a resource centre and a clearing house for money, people, weapons, and ideas moving between the various Islamist groups within and beyond the Muslim countries. Beyond that, there were some tens of thousands of activists fully committed to the struggle, some hundreds of thousands of sympathizers who were trustworthy enough to be depended on for money, shelter, or other services – and tens of millions of Muslims who already shared some of the group's Islamist perspectives and might be moved to more active support by the right combination of pressures. The West's allotted role in al-Qaeda's grand strategy was to supply those pressures (unwittingly, of course) by overreacting to the Islamists' attacks. And they were in no particular hurry: As they put it themselves, "The Americans have all the watches, but we have the time."

The first large terrorist operations that were planned and co-ordinated by al-Qaeda cadres were the simultaneous truck-bomb attacks on US embassies in Kenya and Tanzania in 1998, which killed twelve Americans and 289 African passers-by. Six months before the attacks, bin Laden had cleared his theological flank by issuing a fatwa (an Islamic religious edict) that stated: "The ruling to kill the Americans and their allies – civilians and military – is an individual duty for every Muslim who can do it in any country in which it is possible to do it, in order to liberate the al-Aqsa Mosque [in Jerusalem] and the holy mosque [in Mecca] from their grip, and in order for their armies to move out of all the lands of Islam, defeated and unable to threaten any Muslim." It was not theologically sound, for bin Laden is not a religious authority empowered under Islamic law to deliver a fatwa, but it made the point with the target audience and the words were followed by actions.

Planning and preparation for the 9/11 attacks on the United States began only six months after the East African bombings, and took two and a half years to complete. So focused was al-Qaeda on this single goal that in all that time it only carried out one other operation, a suicide motorboat attack on the destroyer USS *Cole* in Aden harbour in 2000 that killed seventeen American sailors. Taking the time to prepare thoroughly paid off: in the end, the attacks on the World Trade Center towers in New York and the Pentagon in Washington were successful probably even beyond al-Qaeda's expectations, killing almost three thousand Americans and others in a ghastly live-television spectacle that engraved the images of horror in every American's mind and guaranteed a massive American retaliation. Which was precisely what bin Laden wanted.

What did Osama bin Laden expect to gain from the 9/11 attacks? Clearly they would raise the profile of the Islamist cause in the Muslim world and produce some new recruits from amongst the devout and disgruntled young, but in terms of the limited numbers that his training camps could handle there was no shortage of recruits anyway. Just as clearly, it would not bring the United States whimpering to its knees, begging for mercy. Anybody who knew as much about the world as bin Laden would have been well aware that America would strike back massively. If he knew that would be the result, and he went ahead with the attacks anyway, then we must presume that he wanted that result.

What form did he think American retaliation would take? At the very least he would have expected it to match President Bill Clinton's response to the 1998 attacks on US embassies in East Africa, which was to shower al-Qaeda's training camps in Afghanistan with dozens of cruise missiles. Given the far larger casualty toll of 9/11 and the fact that it happened on American soil, however, he would have been expecting and hoping for something more: an American invasion of Afghanistan. He was quite right to do so, as any American president

– Al Gore just as much as George W. Bush – would have been under irresistible popular pressure at home to strike back decisively against the country that sheltered the terrorists who planned those attacks.

He also probably expected that the US armed forces would have the same miserable experience in Afghanistan that the Russians had in the 1980s: an easy entry into the country (which had no defences to speak of), followed by a long and bitter guerrilla war producing significant American casualties and a huge Afghan death toll. Muslims elsewhere, infuriated by this, might then turn to the Islamists and overthrow their pro-American regimes, at least in the Arab world.

But it did not actually happen like that. Rather than rolling into Afghanistan with a couple of hundred thousand frightened young American soldiers who carpeted the landscape with firepower in the good old US Army style to suppress any possible resistance (and thereby caused tens of thousands of innocent Muslim casualties and played into the hands of the Islamists), the Bush administration did it the clever way. They sent in Central Intelligence Agency operatives with suitcases full of cash to buy the loyalty of militias in minority areas in northern Afghanistan who were already in revolt against the Taliban regime, and to buy up some of the Taliban's own local commanders as well. They also sent in Special Forces soldiers to designate targets in the Taliban lines facing the rebels for intense but highly accurate bombardment by the US Air Force. And less than a month after 9/11, the bombing began.

The best estimate for the Afghan death toll during the invasion is under 4,000, most of them combatants, so the images of suffering Muslim innocents blasted by American firepower were not very plentiful and the radicalization of Muslim opinion that Osama bin Laden had sought did not occur. The warlords who sided with the Americans have largely been left in control of the rural areas and even the towns outside of Kabul, which is the main reason why no powerful Afghan resistance movement has yet emerged. Behind the flimsiest of democratic facades, the United States pulled off a classic operation in the high imperial style in Afghanistan, and utterly confounded bin Laden's expectations. The sole Islamist regime in the entire Muslim world was overthrown, and there has not been a single successful Islamist uprising elsewhere.

Moreover, the original al-Qaeda no longer exists in the form that it took between 1996 and 2001 in Afghanistan: its bases are smashed, its people are scattered, and they will never again regroup as a coherent organization. Capturing or killing Osama bin Laden at this point would make little practical difference to the Islamist movement's ability to strike against Western targets. As he said himself shortly after escaping from the American bombing of the Tora Bora caves in late 2001: "If Osama lives or dies does not matter … The awakening has started." How much of an "awakening" ensues, however, is another question. The answer depends largely on how far the United States wades into the trap that he set. Unfortunately – and no doubt to bin Laden's great surprise and delight – President Bush, having dealt with Afghanistan, proceeded to invade Iraq as well.

"When it is over, if it is over, this war will have horrible consequences. Instead of having one [Osama] bin Laden, we will have a hundred."

– Egyptian president Hosni Mubarak, March 2003

The US invasion of Iraq was an enormous stroke of luck for the Islamists, and there will undoubtedly be some hell to pay in the Middle East as a result, but it hasn't solved the basic dilemma of the Islamists. They still do not command the loyalty of enough people in any Arab country to pull off a successful revolution, and their project remains firmly stuck in the mud. Perhaps enough dead Iraqis (plus a healthy helping of dead Palestinians in the occupied territories) will finally drive the people of some Arab country to revolt against their pro-American rulers one of these days, but there are no signs yet of such a movement sweeping the Arab world as a whole, let alone the broader Muslim world.

The Islamists are marginal to Muslim society, and their closest approaches to seizing power by force in major Arab countries – in Egypt, in Syria, in Algeria – may already be behind them. The international terrorism they have gone in for in the past decade is more desperation than anything else, and their long, slow decline will probably continue unless there is a really dramatic boost in the inadvertent help they are getting from the West. Israeli nuclear weapons use on Arab cities, or an American military occupation of Arabia, might do the trick, but short of that the Islamists will probably never even accomplish stage one of their project.

The loosely linked array of Islamist successor groups still known collectively in the West as al-Qaeda has a high nuisance value. Their proven competence at low-tech terrorist attacks makes them a constant, high-profile threat throughout the West, but that just proves that publicity works. They do not threaten either world order or really large numbers of lives, and it is hard to see how they could do so unless they acquired not just one nuclear weapon but a whole arsenal of them. Their greatest international significance is not what they have done themselves or even what they might do, but rather the excuse they have furnished to another small group of determined people with a project to change the world.

CHAPTER III

THE NEO-CONSERVATIVE PROJECT

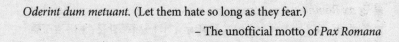

Oderint dum metuant. (Let them hate so long as they fear.)

– The unofficial motto of *Pax Romana*

P*ax Romana*, the Roman peace, was a quite viable project that delivered order over a large area at reasonable cost: Rome directly ruled more than half the population of the known world two thousand years ago, and could collect taxes and recruit soldiers from that very broad power base. Even so, *Pax Romana* really just created a zone of peace and safety within the vast reaches of the empire; Rome was frequently at war on its borders, and did not actually exercise much control beyond them. The Bush administration aimed higher than that.

Pax Britannica was closer to what the neo-conservatives had in mind, since it was an overseas imperial venture that was largely driven by commercial and financial considerations and was often content to settle for indirect rule. However, Britain also had a very broad power base. It ruled about a quarter of the human race at the height of the empire, say between 1857 and 1947, and for the early part of that period it also had between a third and a half of all the industrial capacity on the planet. Moreover, Britain's rulers had relatively modest goals for their empire: they were not ideological missionaries, and did not come around to the idea of implanting British parliamentary institutions in their non-white colonies until the empire was collapsing around their ears.

The original *Pax Americana* was much more benign, for it didn't formally involve an empire at all. It came into existence in the late 1940s, when a visionary generation of American statesmen and soldiers took upon themselves the responsibility of containing Soviet power *without* fighting the Third World War. They made many mistakes along the way, but they helped to rebuild the shattered states of Western Europe and Japan and fostered democracy in them, they created alliances that held the line without frightening the Russians or the Chinese into doing anything foolish – and they also backed the new international institutions that might one day replace the "balance of terror" as a way of running the world. Above all, they were patient, and after forty years their patience was spectacularly rewarded when their main adversary, the Soviet Union, set its own empire free and non-violently metamorphosed into a more or less democratic country. Terrible things were done by both sides in those forty years, but *Pax Americana* delivered the goods: there was no Third World War, and the totalitarians lost. By 1989 or 1990, in fact, the United States had effectively worked itself out of the job of being the "leader of the Free World," for the rival world was also becoming free.

The man who was president of the United States when this great change came, George H.W. Bush, welcomed it as a deliverance and began the process of reshaping American policy for a less confrontational era when the United Nations would finally come into its own and the great powers would co-operate in keeping the peace. There were vested interests in Washington (and in other capitals) that were going to be badly hurt by the end of the Cold War, but they did not seem powerful enough to stem a tide that was sweeping the world. *Pax Americana* was laid to rest, and through the early 1990s defence spending fell sharply in all the industrialized countries: you could practically hear the long sigh of relief as a generation that had lived their entire lives under the threat of a global nuclear war finally grasped that it had really been cancelled. Bad things happened to many innocent people in Rwanda, in former Yugoslavia, in the Caucasus and former Soviet Central Asia, in East

Timor, and in a number of other places – in a world with almost two hundred countries, a few of them are almost bound to be in trouble at any given time – but for the great majority of humankind it was a time of peace and of hope.

It is still a time of peace, actually, in the sense that there are only three or four active wars of any size in the whole world – and it should still be a time of hope too, for nothing has drastically changed since the early 1990s except for a slight rise in the amount of terrorism. (Americans see it as a huge rise in the amount of terrorism, but that is due to one shocking event: in the three years that have passed since 9/11, more Americans have been killed by bolts of lightning than by terrorists.) But hope is not the dominant characteristic of the new century. Many Americans live in fear of a terrorist threat that has been deliberately and grotesquely exaggerated; most of the politically attentive people in the rest of the world live with the growing worry that something is going badly wrong. That something is American foreign policy: *Pax Americana* has been raised from its shallow grave, and it has turned nasty.

The new-model *Pax Americana* is much more ambitious than the original, which was limited to specific geographical areas and essentially defensive in nature. It aims at "full-spectrum dominance" militarily, which requires not only the sort of strategic superiority embodied in nineteenth-century Britain's command of the sea, but overwhelming power everywhere on land as well. "The military must be ready to strike at a moment's notice in any dark corner of the world," President George W. Bush told West Point cadets in 2002. "America has, and intends to keep, military strengths beyond challenge." Moreover, this enormous military strength will be devoted not merely to maintaining order, but to the task of bringing about radical political transformations in a number of non-Western societies, by force if necessary – and since 9/11, the principal focus of that effort has been the Arab world. Tom Friedman, one of the head cheerleaders for the invasion of Iraq at the *New York Times*, wrote in October 2003 that "this is the most radical-liberal revolutionary war that the US has ever launched – a war of choice to install some democracy in the heart of the Arab-Muslim world."

That is a rather tall order for the United States, a country eight thousand miles away where few people are Muslim and hardly anybody speaks Arabic – but then, the new *Pax Americana* project as a whole is a tall order for a country with as narrow a power base as America. The United States spends more on its armed forces than the next nine or ten countries combined, but it doesn't get a lot for its money in terms of usable military power. It has enough nuclear weapons to incinerate the planet several times over, and even without using the nukes it can bomb any country that doesn't have a modern air-defence system with impunity, but it hasn't enough ground troops to occupy a single country of 25 million people effectively, and it probably couldn't go on fighting anywhere once its casualties rose above ten thousand dead: public opinion at home would rebel.

The United States still has the biggest economy in the world, but its share of global gross domestic product (GDP) has declined from a peak of around 50 per cent in 1945 to about 20 per cent in 2005 and a further relative decline is sure to follow, as the biggest Asian economies are currently growing at more than twice the annual rate of the US economy. It is also extremely vulnerable economically because of its huge trade and budget deficits. How did a country with such a fragile power base and so little to gain from establishing military hegemony over the globe – for it already enjoys most of the benefits that might come from having a global economic presence – ever let itself get lured into this foolish adventure?

"The battle for the mind of Ronald Reagan was like the trench warfare of World War I: Never have so many fought so hard for such barren terrain."

– Peggy Noonan, special assistant and
speech writer to Reagan, 1984–88

The founding myth of the neo-conservative project is the belief that Ronald Reagan destroyed the Soviet Union and won the Cold War. He did so, according to the legend, by a combination of huge defence budgets that the Soviet Union could not match and a single magical speech in which he called for the dissolution of the "evil empire" – by a combination, that is, of military and ideological power. The American trumpet sounded, and the walls came tumbling down.

This is a misrepresentation of Ronald Reagan, who was not really a crusader at all. The Star Wars project that allegedly forced the Soviet Union into bankruptcy was in Reagan's mind a genuine attempt to protect the United States from the consequences of a nuclear war – and to the despair of his advisers (who understood that it was really about seeking the ability to carry out a nuclear first strike against the Soviet Union without fear of retaliation), he wanted to share the technology with the Soviet Union. In 1986, at a summit meeting in Iceland, Reagan actually agreed with Soviet leader Mikhail Gorbachev on a plan for getting rid of all the offensive ballistic missiles on both sides, until his refusal to abandon Star Wars wrecked the deal. He did sleepwalk through his presidency, and most of those around him were devoted Cold Warriors, but on the danger of nuclear war, Ronald Reagan's heart was in the right place.

As for the notion that it was the Reagan administration's decisions that destroyed the communist empire, that is a huge misunderstanding of what really happened. The Soviet command economy virtually stopped growing after the mid-1960s because of its own internal failings, but Soviet defence spending, always a bigger share of a much smaller economy, continued to track that of the United States, whose economy continued to grow. The Nixon and Carter defence budgets of the 1970s grew only slowly, but by 1980 the cumulative impact on Soviet military spending of trying to keep up was huge: defence spending was taking up to 30 to 35 per cent of the Soviet economy. Reagan increased the US defence spending sharply beginning with his own first defence budget in 1982, but that came so late in the game that it was practically irrelevant: he was flogging a horse that was already dead.

The growing economic crisis in the Soviet system was masked throughout the 1970s by the very high price the country was getting for its oil exports, which brought in enough foreign exchange to sustain the reward system by which the regime bought the loyalty of the key 10 or 15 per cent of the population. When oil prices fell drastically in 1981–82, the foreign exchange dried up and an attempt at root-and-branch economic reforms became unavoidable – all this well before there had been time for Reagan's bigger defence budget to have any significant impact.

But the whole Soviet system was so rotten and overstretched that as soon as Gorbachev's economic reforms began to bite, it started coming apart at the seams. That drove Gorbachev to offer political reforms as well, in a last-ditch attempt to save communism, but it was too little, too late, and the whole system collapsed non-violently between 1989 and 1991.

"The Soviet people want full-blooded and unconditional democracy."
– Mikhail Gorbachev, 1988

By the end of Reagan's second term in 1988, foreigners who spent a lot of time with the democratic opposition in Russia could see that communist rule was really drawing to a close, though it still seemed an astonishing idea. However, there is no evidence that anyone in the Reagan administration actually saw it coming. In fact, they didn't notice that the Soviet Union was changing at all for a full year and a half after Gorbachev had come to power in 1985 – but then the Iran-Contra scandal broke at the end of 1986, implicating Reagan's close associates and advisers in a bizarre and highly illegal scheme to sell arms to Iran (despite the fact that his administration supported Saddam Hussein's attack on Iran at the same time), and to use the proceeds of these arms sales to fund guerrilla attacks on the Nicaraguan government.

Reagan escaped formal censure by insisting that he could not remember if anybody had ever mentioned it to him, but he was in desperate trouble politically, and one way of diverting attention from the unfolding scandal was to change tack on the "evil empire" and begin a high-profile courtship of Mikhail Gorbachev. The Soviet leader was more than ready to respond, and within a year the two men had become almost dependent on each other for their popularity with their respective domestic audiences: on his visit to Moscow in 1988, Reagan said that his talk of an evil empire was from "another time." But when Ronald Reagan left office at the end of that year, neither he nor any of his associates had the slightest inkling that the Soviet Union was just three years away from collapse. Communism fell of its own weight, and they just claimed credit for it after the fact.

Some of the more far-sighted members of the Reagan administration and the subsequent administration of George H.W. Bush did, however, grasp a new and unwelcome reality: when the Soviet Union finally died in 1991, so did the need for *Pax Americana*, at least as far as other countries were concerned. If the United States wanted to go on being the paramount power – if it even wanted to maintain its existing pattern of defence spending – it would have to find some new enemies.

"Institutions like to continue what they have been doing, always on a grander scale, if possible. When old enemies disappear, mellow or turn into allies, as frequently happens in international relations, new enemies must be found and new threats must be discovered. The failure to replenish the supply of enemies is the supreme threat facing any national security bureaucracy."

– Richard J. Barnet, *Roots of War* (1971)

By the start of the 1990s, it was already an unshakable part of American political mythology that Ronald Reagan had brought down the Soviet Union, and by extension that a combination of US military power and the irresistible attraction of American political values could bring about huge transformations in other people's societies. It was not too long a journey from that belief to the conclusion that the United States could and should use these same assets to remake the whole world in its own image – a transformation that would, in the eyes of most Americans, simultaneously do everybody else a favour and make the world a safer place for Americans. This would require the renewal and refounding of *Pax Americana* on a much more unilateral basis, but there were lots of people in Washington who could live with that.

In official Washington in the early 1990s, there was a desperate scramble for a new rationale to sustain the patterns of military spending (including think-tank contracts) that had become normal during forty years of Cold War. Two whole generations of professional soldiers and civilian defence experts had devoted their careers to coping with the immense threat presented by the Soviet Union, and suddenly it wasn't there any more – but it was too late to change career, and families still had to be fed, so a frantic search began for some new threat or threats that could sustain the existing pattern of expenditure.

Terrorism certainly wasn't a big enough threat to justify defence budgets on a Cold War scale in the early 1990s (and it still isn't), so in the absence of plausible great-power enemies the default option was "rogue states." North Korea, Syria, Iraq, Iran, and Libya had all been under the same management for between ten and forty years at this point, and their regimes had all been much more hostile towards the United States in their early years than they were by the early 1990s, but suddenly, for want of anything better, they were promoted to the first rank of global threats. Of course, they couldn't really be inflated enough to fill the space vacated by the Soviet Union unless they, too, were able to attack the United States with nuclear weapons, so suddenly that also became a concern.

"If we were truly realistic instead of idealistic, as we appear to be, we would not permit any foreign power with which we are not firmly allied, and in which we do not have absolute confidence, to make or possess nuclear weapons. If such a country started to make atomic weapons we would destroy its capacity to make them before it has progressed far enough to threaten us."

– General Leslie Groves, head of the
Manhattan Project, October 1945

Leslie Groves was usually viewed as barking mad when he advocated attacking other countries that tried to obtain nuclear weapons, but almost half a century later, in a capital where a lot of good jobs were at risk, the people who gradually became known as the neo-conservatives got a much warmer reception. "Rogue states" with "weapons of mass destruction" became the new obsession – and what was so neat about them was that you weren't just confined to "defensive measures" like pouring money into the ever-popular Ballistic Missile Defense programme. Because they were small and vulnerable countries, you could design forces (very expensive forces) for "going after them" and "taking them out." Pre-emptive war (to forestall an impending attack) and preventive war (to destroy a potential future threat) both became possible strategies in a way that they had never been against the Soviet Union – and on this foundation began to be built a project for the perpetuation of US global domination based on the unilateral exercise of over-whelming American power. The first people to succumb to this fantasy were mostly men who had worked in the Reagan adminis-tration and were amazed by what they thought (in retrospect) that they had wrought. Men like Dick Cheney, Paul Wolfowitz, and Lewis "Scooter" Libby.

In the spring of 1992, when Cheney was secretary of defense in President George H.W. Bush's administration and Wolfowitz and Libby were relatively junior political appointees at the Pentagon, excerpts from a draft "Defense Planning Guidance" written by the latter two men were leaked to the *New York Times* and led a horri-fied Democratic senator, Joseph Biden, to denounce the document as a prescription "literally for a *Pax Americana*." Written in the after-math of America's easy victory in the Gulf War of 1990–91, the doc-ument proposed a new strategy "to set the nation's direction for the next century" in which unchallengeable American military power would "establish and protect a new order" – but this was not the elder President Bush's idea of a New World Order built around great-power collaboration under the authority of the United Nations.

The Wolfowitz–Libby "Defense Planning Guidance" did not even mention the UN, and called for permanent American military pre-eminence over all of Europe and Asia, including the Middle East. The United States must be capable of "deterring potential competitors from even aspiring to a larger regional or global role," including current allies like Germany and Japan, and it must be willing to use pre-emptive force against states that it suspected of developing weapons of mass destruction. US military intervention overseas would be a "constant feature" in the future, and it might well include the pre-emptive use of American nuclear, biological, and chemical weapons.

It was an ultra-radical, some would say half-crazed, manifesto for American world domination that had no place in an administration as conventional and conservative as that of George Bush Sr., and although it had presumably been written with Dick Cheney's encouragement, saner members of the administration, like Secretary of State James Baker and National Security Adviser Brent Scowcroft, successfully insisted that the document undergo radical surgery. Like George Bush Sr. himself, Baker and Scowcroft were old-guard Republicans with extensive international experience who believed that even American power was limited, and that the best way of maximizing US influence in the world was usually to work through multilateral institutions within the framework of international law. But they all got dumped together when the Democrats returned to the White House under Bill Clinton at the end of 1992, and the proponents of a new and far more sweeping version of *Pax Americana* spent the next eight years gnashing their teeth in the outer darkness while the great opportunity, as they saw it, passed America by. No sooner had history opened the door to them than American voters closed it again.

But the temptation to go it alone was great and growing in a world where the sudden collapse of the Soviet Union meant that the United States, for the moment, was the one and only superpower, and Cheney, Wolfowitz, and Libby were not alone in their conviction that the United States should seize the "unipolar moment." In their long but comfortable exile from active politics in 1993–2000, they gathered allies, mostly former Reagan and Bush administration officials now working in the oil and defence industries or roosting in various hard-right think-tanks in Washington – and their enforced holiday from government gave them the time and the freedom for a well-coordinated ideological campaign that eventually led to a sharp radicalization in thinking on defence and foreign policy in the upper ranks of the Republican Party. Ironically, they were known as neo-conservatives.

The *neo* refers to the fact that many of the original neo-conservative inner circle began their careers as Democrats, although hardly mainstream members of the Democratic Party. Paul Wolfowitz, deputy defense secretary in George W. Bush's first administration; Richard Perle, who served as chair of the Defense Policy Board until allegations of conflict of interest forced him out in 2003; Douglas Feith, undersecretary of defense for policy; and Elliott Abrams, deputy national security adviser with special responsibility for the Middle East and the "global democracy" project, all served on the staff of Democratic Senator Henry "Scoop" Jackson in the 1970s, at a time when Jackson was the most hawkish Cold Warrior in the Senate. (His major legislative contribution in that period was the Jackson–Vanik Amendment, which required freedom of emigration in US trading partners as a precondition of normal trade relations with the United States. Its main purpose and practical effect was to open the door to the mass emigration of Soviet Jews to Israel.) Wolfowitz, Perle, Feith, and Abrams all have long-standing links with the hard-line Likud bloc in Israel, and Perle and Feith collaborated in a 1996 study for incoming Likud prime minister Binyamin Netanyahu entitled *A Clean Break*, which prominently advocated the overthrow of Saddam Hussein in Iraq as an essential part of a new Israeli strategy that would break out of the constraints of the Oslo Accords.

A year later, on June 3, 1997, Wolfowitz and Abrams, together with William Kristol and Robert Kagan (co-founders of the neo-conservative house organ *The Weekly Standard*), Dick Cheney (later vice-president under George W. Bush), Lewis "Scooter" Libby (later Cheney's chief of staff), Donald Rumsfeld (defense secretary), Peter Rodman (assistant secretary of defense for international security affairs), Paula Dobriansky (undersecretary of state for global affairs), Zalmay Khalilzad (US ambassador to Afghanistan and

Iraq), and Jeb Bush (governor of Florida, but perhaps more importantly George W. Bush's younger brother), signed the statement of principles of a new pressure group, the Project for a New American Century (PNAC). The PNAC's goal was "to shape a new century favourable to American principles and interests," and the way to do that was to return to what they held to be the policies of the Reagan years: "A Reaganite policy of military strength and moral clarity may not be fashionable today. But it is necessary if the US is to build on the success of this past century and ensure our security and greatness in the next."

What did that actually mean? Part of the answer came in the open letter that the PNAC founders, plus new members Richard Perle and John Bolton (undersecretary of state for arms control and international security in the first Bush administration and now US ambassador to the United Nations) and some other like-minded signatories, including James Woolsey (former director of the Central Intelligence Agency and a member of the Defense Policy Board under Bush), wrote to President Bill Clinton on January 26, 1998. They urged him to adopt a new policy aimed at "the removal of Saddam Hussein's regime from power," because otherwise "the safety of American troops in the region, of our friends and allies like Israel and the moderate Arab states, and a significant portion of the world's supply of oil will all be put at hazard." The broader strategy behind the Iraq recommendation was first sketched out in an article, "Towards a Neo-Reaganite Foreign Policy," that Kristol and Kagan published in *Foreign Affairs* in 1996, in which they argued that the United States should seize the "unipolar moment" when it was the only superpower, and adopt policies that would extend its exalted status indefinitely. A resurrected *Pax Americana*, in other words.

The Project for a New American Century advocated preemptive military attacks on "rogue states" like North Korea, Iran, and Iraq, and reorientation of America's political and military strategy from the old enemy, Russia, to the emerging strategic rival, China. It could easily have been the late nineteenth century, when British pressure groups were urging a reorientation of the country's defence efforts from the old enemy, France, to the new challenger, Germany. Indeed, so far as the neo-conservatives were concerned, it *was* the late nineteenth century, with not a moment's thought given to multilateral and non-military ways of dealing with the problem of changing power relationships. As they put it in their open letter to President Clinton, "American policy cannot continue to be crippled by a misguided insistence on unanimity in the UN security council."

The last and most complete statement of the PNAC's vision for a unipolar, American-run world before the responsibilities of office forced its members to stop talking openly about their ultimate objectives was a document produced in September 2000 entitled *Rebuilding America's Defenses: Strategy, Forces and Resources for a New Century*. It began: "The United States is the world's only super-power, combining preeminent military power, global technological leadership, and the world's largest economy ... America's grand strategy should aim to preserve and extend this advantageous position as far into the future as possible ... Yet no moment in international politics can be frozen in time; even a global *Pax Americana* will not preserve itself."

So how could the United States extend this moment as far as possible into the future? The report advocated establishing an unchallengeable nuclear superiority based on "a new family" of more usable nuclear weapons, the restructuring of the air force "toward a global first-strike force," and the development and deployment of "global missile defenses to defend the American homeland ... and to provide a secure basis for US power projection around the world." The Anti-Ballistic Missile Treaty must therefore be torn up, since the prerequisite for an American nuclear first-strike capability was the ability to prevent target nations from retaliating against the United States with nuclear weapons. The United States should also "control the new 'international commons' of space and 'cyber-space,' and pave the way for the creation of a new military service – US Space Forces – with the mission of space control."

On the ground, there must be enough American combat forces to fight and win multiple major wars at the same time. This would be made possible at an affordable cost by rapid exploitation of the "revolution in military affairs" (the move to high-tech, unmanned weaponry) "to insure the long-term superiority of US conventional forces," and by the establishment of "a network of 'deployment bases' or 'forward operating bases' to increase the reach of current and proposed forces." Substantial US forces would have to be based abroad to fulfil "multiple constabulary missions" around the world, and these forces should remain under American rather than UN command. "The presence of American forces in critical regions around the world is the visible expression of the extent of America's status as a superpower," the document argued, and the United States must not allow "North Korea, Iran, Iraq or similar states to undermine American leadership, intimidate American allies, or threaten the American homeland itself." In this way, it would be possible to "preserve *Pax Americana*" and a "unipolar 21st century."

On the specific question of the Gulf region, the PNAC document was remarkably frank about what an attack on Iraq should lead to: "While the unresolved conflict with Iraq provides the immediate justification, the need for a substantial American force presence in the Gulf transcends the issue of the regime of Saddam Hussein." The wider strategic aim was "maintaining global US preeminence," which would be greatly enhanced by American control of the Persian Gulf oilfields, the main source of oil imports for the emerging Chinese industrial giant, since a principal purpose of the massive military build-up would be "to cope with the rise of China to great-power status." But although they were only months away from an election that could return a Republican president to the White House, the authors of *Rebuilding America's Defenses* were remarkably pessimistic about the likelihood that their project would be translated into policy any time soon, "absent some catastrophic and catalyzing event – like a new Pearl Harbor."

Such were the views of the neo-conservatives on the brink of taking power in the United States – and *none* of this discussion was taking place in the context of a "war on terror." It was a programme for American global hegemony, and they were working hard to ensure that it could be done at a cost reasonable enough not to alienate American voters. It was not a conspiracy: the neo-conservatives, far from hiding their views and their ties, actively campaigned for their project. It did logically require the marginalization of the United Nations and it called for some wars that would probably be illegal within the existing structure of international law, but America's veto on the Security Council (like that of the other traditional great powers) existed precisely to exempt it from the UN's rules and from international law whenever it felt the need.

So it was an entirely viable project, at least in the short term, if the American public could be persuaded to back it. The only worry that might have clouded the day for historically conscious neo-conservatives was the fact that the kind of massive military reorganization they were proposing to underpin *Pax Americana* had only been undertaken in the case of its predecessors, *Pax Romana* and *Pax Britannica*, when the power of the empire in question was already slipping into irreversible decline.

"History is replete with examples of empires mounting impressive military campaigns on the cusp of their impending economic collapse."

– Eric Alterman, *Sound and Fury: The Washington Punditocracy and the Collapse of American Politics* (1992)

This is the point, just before Bush and the neo-conservatives take office at the beginning of 2001, where the answers to some key questions about the nature and purposes of the *Pax Americana* project become clear. First, the "big" conspiracy theory that Emmanuel Todd raised in his book, *Après l'empire*: Is the entire enterprise of reviving *Pax Americana*, this time on a truly global basis, really just a diversionary operation, intended to impress the world with America's strategic indispensability and military invincibility in order to distract attention from its extreme economic vulnerability? And is it, by the way, a bipartisan project? When you put it like that, it sounds pretty silly – and that suggests that it probably is.

There was certainly a shift in the American public mood towards impatience with international institutions and a growing obsession with America's military power as the 1990s neared their end. That mood was reflected in Clinton's last defence budgets, which started going back up after 1998, as well as in his inability to get such innocuous multilateral agreements as the land-mines treaty and the International Criminal Court accepted by Congress and his own military. But the Democrats showed no interest in a resurrected *Pax Americana* while Clinton was in office.

The fact that a lot of them voted in 2002 for Bush's invasion of Iraq only proves that they were either gullible (and believed the cooked intelligence that they were served) or extremely cynical (and believed that they were giving Bush enough rope to hang himself). In the case of Senate Majority leader Tom Daschle and Senator John Kerry it was unquestionably the latter: they consistently and successfully argued that to attack Bush on the "war on terror," civil liberties, or the invasion of Iraq would be to walk into the trap set by Karl Rove, the president's political strategist. If Bush's war prospered, he would win the next election anyway; if it did not, at least the Republicans would not be able to blame the failure on the Democrats. There was no bipartisan conspiracy to recreate *Pax Americana*.

Very well, then, was there at least a Republican conspiracy that saw *Pax Americana* as a necessary strategy to deal with America's economic weakness? Almost certainly not. The feet of clay beneath the US economy today are the huge foreign trade deficit and the equally huge budget deficit, but only one of those feet had yet turned to clay in the late 1990s. The trade deficit began to soar in the last few years of the decade, but the Clinton administration had successfully wrestled the huge budget deficits inherited from the Reagan and the first Bush administrations to the ground. It is the *combination* of the two deficits that creates such an unstable and dangerous situation, and that only came into being after the younger Bush administration came into office.

None of the members of the Bush cabinet with the exception of Treasury Secretary Paul O'Neill (who was sacked for his temerity) ever said anything in public that suggested they were even dimly aware of the gravity of the problem. Indeed, it is unimaginable that they would have voluntarily created a massive budget deficit with their tax cuts if they had even understood the nature of the problem. What drove *Pax Americana* was hubris, not economics. And certainly not terrorism.

CHAPTER IV

TARGET IRAQ

"I expected to go back to a round of meetings [on September 12, 2001] examining what the next attacks could be, what our vulnerabilities were, what we could do about them in the short term. Instead, I walked into a series of discussions about Iraq. At first I was incredulous that we were talking about something other than getting al Qaeda. Then I realized with almost a sharp physical pain that Rumsfeld and Wolfowitz were going to try to take advantage of this national tragedy to promote their agenda about Iraq. Since the beginning of the administration, indeed well before, they had been pressing for a war with Iraq. My friends in the Pentagon had been telling me that the word was we would be invading Iraq sometime in 2002."

– Former White House counter-terrorism chief
Richard A. Clarke, *Against All Enemies* (2004)

If there were no "rogue states" in the world, and no "weapons of mass destruction" either, 9/11 would have happened in just the same way. Only one day after 9/11, the Central Intelligence Agency (CIA) was already certain that al-Qaeda had sponsored the attacks, but to counter-terrorism chief Richard A. Clarke's dismay Paul Wolfowitz, deputy to Defense Secretary Donald Rumsfeld, was insisting that such a sophisticated operation must have had a state sponsor. His candidate for the guilty party was, of course, Iraq. By the following day, Rumsfeld was talking about "getting" Iraq: "[He] complained that there were no decent targets for bombing in Afghanistan and that we should consider bombing Iraq, which, he said, had better targets. At first I thought Rumsfeld was joking. But he was serious and the President did not reject out of hand the idea of attacking Iraq. Instead he noted that what we needed to do with Iraq was to change the regime, not just hit it with more cruise missiles ..."

We now know that the Bush administration came into office already determined to invade Iraq: former treasury secretary Paul O'Neill has revealed that at the very first meeting of President Bush's National Security Committee (NSC) on January 30, 2001, more than seven months before the terrorist attacks on 9/11, the invasion of Iraq was "Topic A." In an interview with CBS News in January 2004 that coincided with the publication of *The Price of*

Loyalty: George W. Bush, the White House, and the Education of Paul O'Neill, a book by journalist Ron Suskind that chronicled the former treasury secretary's two years in the Bush cabinet, O'Neill said, "From the very first instance, it was about Iraq. It was all about finding a way to do it. That was the tone of it: the President saying, 'Go find me a way to do this.'" Within weeks O'Neill saw a secret dossier entitled "Plan for post-Saddam Iraq," and an attack on Iraq remained an abiding theme in subsequent NSC meetings. Indeed, reports O'Neill, nobody questioned the assumption that Iraq should be invaded, and even the calamity of 9/11 did not derail the neo-conservatives' fixation on Iraq. They simply appropriated the terrorist attack as a convenient vehicle for pursuing it.

But why were they so determined to invade Iraq? On the face of it, it made no sense, for Iraq wasn't threatening anybody. It had been under strict UN embargo since the end of the Gulf War in 1991, and Saddam Hussein was just barely managing to stay afloat. He wasn't even particularly hostile to the United States: Saddam came to be seen as a dangerous enemy by Washington after his monumental blunder in invading Kuwait in 1990, but he had been quite happy to be an informal ally of the United States during his war against Iran in the 1980s, and seems genuinely not to have understood that his invasion of Kuwait would irreparably damage that relationship. (The record of his interview with US ambassador April Glaspie just before the invasion strongly suggests that he was seeking a green light from Washington, and may have mistakenly concluded that he had got it.) Even after his defeat in the Gulf War of 1991, he had no motive to sponsor terrorist attacks against the United States, and every reason to avoid doing so in view of the likely retaliation. The White House's own counter-terrorism expert and the CIA would both have told Bush and his cabinet colleagues, if they had cared to inquire, that Iraq was not involved in supporting anti-US terrorist activities. If they were concerned about terrorism, al-Qaeda was the one to worry about.

But they weren't concerned about terrorism. Richard A. Clarke recounts in his book *Against All Enemies* that it took him more than seven months from the time of his first request, until only a week before 9/11, to get an opportunity to address the Principals Committee (Vice-President Dick Cheney, Secretary of Defense Donald Rumsfeld, Secretary of State Colin Powell, National Security Adviser Condoleezza Rice, and the heads of the CIA and the FBI) on the threat from al-Qaeda. And the Bush administration wasn't really concerned about allegations of weapons of mass destruction in Iraq at this point either: the extent to which it finally ended up believing its own cooked intelligence about Iraq's mythical weapons of mass destruction is debatable, but the subject was not even on the table during the seven months before 9/11. The administration's foreign priorities at that time were focused on ideological issues – withdrawing from the Kyoto treaty on climate change, sabotaging the International Criminal Court, killing proposals for controlling the global trade in small arms and for strengthening the Biological Weapons Convention – and on global hegemony issues like getting the Ballistic Missile Defense programme up and running (which required withdrawing from the Anti-Ballistic Missile Treaty). So again, why Iraq?

Popular wisdom may cynically believe that "it's all about oil," but it actually isn't. The notion of "strategic security of oil supply," if it ever had any validity, lost it at the end of the Cold War. Nobody is going to blockade or sink the tankers bringing oil to the consumers, and the producers themselves simply cannot afford to stop pumping the stuff and selling it to all comers: their people live off the proceeds. The Iranian regime may hate the Great Satan, but Iran has pumped oil right up to the limit imposed by the Organization of Petroleum Exporting Countries (OPEC) cartel every month since the revolution in 1979 (and often beyond the limit), and willingly sold it to any Western country that wanted to buy it at the going market price. How else is it going to pay for the shiploads of frozen Australian lamb that sail up the Gulf most days to feed 70 million Iranians? You don't have to occupy oil-producing countries militarily at vast expense to get oil from them, you just write them a cheque: Saddam Hussein sold half of Iraq's oil exports to the United States (which was busy filling its strategic reserve in anticipation of the war) the month before the United States invaded Iraq. And as for keeping the oil price down: when did it become an interest of the US oil industry, Bush's closest political ally, to keep the oil price down?

Two other oil-related explanations – that military control over Gulf oil supplies would be a strategic asset for the United States in a future confrontation with China, and that oil concessions in a conquered Iraq would allow the Bush administration to reward its major contributors in the US oil industry – hold a considerable amount of water, given the strategic obsessions of the neo-conservatives and the Bush administration's close, almost symbiotic relationship with the US energy industry. But nobody would invade an entire country out of the blue solely to improve America's future ability to exert strategic pressure on China or to reward campaign contributors.

You can think of other reasons that might have been important in persuading this or that member of the administration to get on the "attack Iraq" bandwagon. The advantages to Israel of crushing that country's strongest remaining Arab opponent would have appealed to the members of the administration who had very close links to the ruling Likud Party in Israel. In a more tangled and arcane way, it would also have appealed to the radical Christian fundamentalists in the Republican core constituency who see the United States and Israel as players fulfilling the Biblical prophecies that herald the End Times. The desirability of acquiring an alternative military base in the Gulf that would allow US troops to be withdrawn from Saudi

Arabia, where they were a permanent irritant to Muslim sensibilities, has also been advanced as a motive for invading Iraq (though it isn't clear why the United States couldn't just have moved the troops from Saudi Arabia to its existing bases in Qatar and Bahrain without the nuisance of a war). Then there are the supposed personal motives, like Bush's desire to take revenge for an alleged plot by Saddam to assassinate his father in 1993, or alternatively an almost Oedipal eagerness by George W. to demonstrate that he could do what his father couldn't – take Baghdad.

Assembling a coalition of people committed to a common goal, even within a group as ideologically focused as the Bush administration, always involves playing on the specific motives that most appeal to the various individuals who must agree. But none of these motives, singly or in combination, could have persuaded this large group of Washington insiders to back such a dramatic and politically risky initiative as an unprovoked invasion of a country in an explosive region halfway round the world. So what over-arching motive did unite them, or at least enough of them to get this project off the ground?

Given what we know about neo-conservative ideas, *Pax Americana* is the obvious candidate. With the exception of former Secretary of State Colin Powell, virtually every senior political appointee dealing with defence and foreign policy in the first Bush administration was associated with various neo-conservative studies and projects. And the main reason that this group had already been agitating publicly for an invasion of Iraq since at least 1996 was that they saw it as the ideal vehicle for relaunching *Pax Americana* on a new basis. They would never have put it that way in public – you can't tell the American public that you want their sons and daughters to die in a war overseas for something as abstract as global hegemony – but they were clever and experienced enough to understand that when you set out to change the global rules, you need to do something dramatic to get people's attention. The cheapest thing to do, in terms of the federal budget and of American lives, was Iraq.

Consider the problem. The old version of *Pax Americana* rarely resorted to naked compulsion. There were exceptions, but successive administrations generally preferred to work through alliances and multilateral organizations under the shelter of international law whenever possible. (It multiplies your leverage, and it annoys people less.) America's hegemony did not extend to the communist-ruled third of the world, of course, nor did Washington bother to exercise it in those parts of the Third World that were not strategically or economically important to it, but the United States genuinely filled the role of paramount power in the industrialized West, still the world's economic heartland. Moreover, its power was generally accepted as a Good Thing (despite much grumbling), because most people in the West believed that there was a real clash of values in the Cold War and that America better represented their values. America's power was never greater or less questioned than when it faced the Soviet Union across a divided world.

Then came the collapse of the Soviet Union, and by purely military and economic measures America's relative power grew even greater. But at the same time American global power faced a crisis of legitimacy, because with the collapse of authoritarian regimes not only in communist-ruled Europe but in major Asian countries and in apartheid South Africa between 1986 and 1994, the United States could no longer convincingly portray itself as the sole guardian of freedom. Democracy was winning all over the place, without American help for the most part, and there was no longer some great and universally feared enemy of freedom against whom Washington could rally the troops. So what would become of the international leadership role that had been such a long and pleasant part of the lives of those who govern in Washington?

The end of the Cold War destroyed the basis for the existing version of *Pax Americana*, but at the same time it seemed to enhance America's relative military power to the point where no other country in the world could defy it. (This was not really true, but most people in Washington believed it.) For those in Washington who want to "preserve and extend this advantageous position as far as possible into the future," the task was therefore to find a new rationale for America's immense military effort and its worldwide military presence. The "rogue states with WMD" story might work with the US domestic audience, but it just wouldn't fly with other governments. In fact, there was *no* cover story that they would swallow: they would just have to be shown who was in charge. The old *Pax Americana* had been compatible with international law and a consultative relationship with America's major allies; the new version would be based much more frankly on naked American power. Perpetuating the "unipolar moment" meant bigger US military budgets than during the Cold War, not smaller, and an effective end to the old consultative alliances like NATO (though the facade might be usefully preserved). More urgently, it required the removal of the restraints imposed by existing laws and treaties: the United States must be free to use its power unilaterally as it wished.

So how could the neo-conservatives let the world know in a dramatic but economical way that the rules have just changed and now the United States is in sole charge? One good way would be to pick some country that has repeatedly defied the United States in the past – but isn't actually attacking it right now, for we don't want this to look like mere retaliation – and to whack it very hard. Create a horrible example of what happens to those who get out of line, in other words.

But won't such an action look capricious? In fact, won't it actually be illegal under existing international law? Yes, of course, but that's fine; we *want* to let the world know that the rules have changed. We need to send a message to everybody that we are in charge now, and further defiance will not be tolerated.

The war mustn't be too difficult, however, because the American public is not up for a bloodbath. The United States, unlike the Roman Empire, is a democracy, and American voters are famous for disliking foreign wars that aren't about the country's survival but still send their kids home in body bags. (They don't like high taxes either, which also tend to be a consequence of foreign wars sooner or later.) So which of the countries that regularly defy the United States could fill the role of horrible example without being too hard to take down?

Several countries qualified as candidates for the treatment on the grounds that they were generally defiant but not currently aggressive. Knocking off North Korea, for example, would make a profound impression on all the other countries in the world, and since the Pyongyang regime was a well-established bogeyman in the US media, invading it wouldn't be too hard a sale to make at home. The problem here was that the North Korean regime might have nuclear weapons. They couldn't reach the United States, of course, but unless American forces could get every one of them in a surprise first strike, Pyongyang's "revenge from the grave" (as the nuclear strategists put it) might destroy Seoul or even Tokyo. It would also be a very big war on the ground, and China's reaction to an American act of aggression on this scale right on its own borders was impossible to calculate. All things considered, North Korea was not the ideal candidate.

How about Iran, then? Iranians officially hated the "Great Satan" and Americans unofficially hated them, and Iran certainly qualified on the defiance scale. Tehran had done nothing particularly aggressive towards the United States in recent years, so it fitted the parameters in terms of non-provocation too. But there were two large drawbacks to attacking Iran. One was that it is full of mountains –

sort of Afghanistan West, except richer, more urbanized, and much more sophisticated. The other was that it is full of Iranians, and there was absolutely no doubt that most of the 70 million Iranians would fight back if America invaded. Maybe Iran wasn't such a good idea either.

Well, then, how about Iraq? It's dead flat, for a start (apart from the northern Kurdish bit, which the United States already controlled). It's good tank country – and there's a lot of oil under that sand, which is a nice bonus. There are only 25 million Iraqis, and their ruler, Saddam Hussein, is a loathsome thug whom nobody loves, so they probably won't fight very hard to save him. Israel sees Iraq under Saddam Hussein as one of its most dangerous enemies, so attacking it will have a special appeal for the Likudniks among the neo-conservatives. And Iraq doesn't have nuclear weapons.

Iraq practically nominated itself. From the earliest moments when the neo-conservatives began to consider how to refound *Pax Americana* as a go-it-alone American project for the New Century, Iraq was at the top of their hit list – not because it was dangerous, but because it wasn't. Invading Iraq wasn't about terrorism, and it wasn't about WMD either; it was about sending the right message to the rest of the world without spending too much in American lives and money to get the message out. All the key foreign policy and defence players in the Bush administration (except Colin Powell) seem to have agreed on that from the first meeting of the National Security Committee in January 2001. The trick was to get the American public to go along with it, because nobody had so much as mentioned attacking Iraq in the election campaign recently past. Of course they hadn't. They would have lost the election.

The problem that faced the neo-conservatives after the election was that they had to send different messages to two different audiences. They had to come up with some argument that would persuade the American public that it was necessary to invade Iraq to protect the United States, while at the same time making it clear to other governments that Washington was unilaterally changing the rules by which the world worked. Other governments would get the message loud and clear if the United States invaded Iraq without any provocation, but that same lack of provocation would make it much harder to sell the war politically at home – especially if Saddam Hussein just sat there and didn't attack any foreign countries, which had been his behaviour for the past ten years. The sheer intractability of this problem may explain why the question of attacking Iraq came up at most of the National Security Committee meetings between January and September 2001, and yet little was actually done about it beyond an updating of military plans. Time passed, treaties got torn up, and work on eliminating the budget surplus went ahead urgently, but the administration made little visible effort to prepare the American public for an invasion of Iraq.

Maybe it was just the press of other business: after eight years' exile from the White House, Republicans had a lot of friends to reward and enemies to punish, which took time. But there is also the possibility that even the devout neo-conservatives in the administration were daunted by the task of manufacturing a completely fake case for invading Iraq in the relatively calm and unthreatening atmosphere that prevailed in the months before 9/11. On the other hand, they sincerely believed that their project was for the long-term benefit of the United States, so they kept the question of Iraq on the table while they tried to figure out a way to sell an invasion to the American people.

"The United States is the best and fairest and most decent nation on the face of the earth."

– George H.W. Bush, 1988

"We know how good we are."

– George W. Bush, 2002

"If we ever pass out as a great nation we ought to put on our tombstone 'America died from a delusion that she had moral leadership.'"

– Will Rogers, 1949

It is a peculiarity of American politics that foreign wars must be sold not in terms of strategic necessity but on moral grounds. This emphasis on moral principle is one of the most attractive aspects of American public life when it does not descend into mere sectarian dogmatism, but it does make it easier to sell wars to Americans.

Ivo H. Daalder and James M. Lindsay, in their book *America Unbound: The Bush Revolution in Foreign Policy*, make a careful distinction between ideologically oriented neo-conservatives and what they call "assertive nationalists," traditional hard-line conservatives who, in their view, include Bush, Cheney, and Rumsfeld. But it is a distinction without a difference, for nationalism, in its American version, is based on a value system that most Americans believe to be of universal relevance. They are right too, but it is very easy for Americans to confuse the nationalist and the universalist parts of it.

Most Americans do not even believe that they are nationalists; they see themselves instead as "patriots." In American eyes, nationalism is a narrow, backward-looking ethnic obsession, mired in old history and old grudges, that immigrants were expected to leave behind when they came to the United States. The American identity is founded not on common ethnicity but on shared democratic ideals. "There is no American race, but there is an American creed," as President Bush said in his Fourth of July speech in 2002. This ideological definition of American identity actually predates the beginning of mass immigration from non-British sources, going all the way back to the Revolutionary War, but it has subsequently been linked in American political rhetoric with the "melting pot" phenomenon of many ethnicities sharing the same society.

It is a very attractive ideology, and far less exclusively American these days than most Americans realize. The richer European countries, Canada, Australia, and New Zealand, thanks to decades of open immigration policies, now have populations whose ethnic variety approaches or even exceeds that of the United States, and their successes and failures in dealing with the resulting challenges are not very different from America's. But in Canada or France or Sweden, national identity in the early twenty-first century is an amalgam of local history and universal human values. Nobody thinks that they hold the copyright on those values, or that their particular mixture of universal values, local history, and local geography is a model for all humankind.

American national identity does aspire to universality, for understandable historical reasons: more than two centuries ago, the American colonies were the first society of more than one million people in human history to create a democratic and egalitarian society. But they didn't come up with the idea themselves: the revolutionary generation of the American "founding fathers," remarkable though they were, drew on a century of intellectual ferment in Europe, and a more radical and arguably more influential revolution broke out in Europe's most powerful country, France, only six years after the United States won its independence. But most Americans genuinely believe that their own revolution was the turning point of world history, and that the United States is, in former secretary of state Madeleine Albright's phrase, the "indispensable nation." This has led to certain unfortunate consequences.

The first is that it disguises the depth and intensity of American nationalism from Americans themselves, because they have been taught that nationalism is a retrograde ethnic phenomenon and that their shared ideals of "freedom" and "equal opportunity" somehow fulfil a different function. In fact, they serve exactly the same function of uniting huge numbers of disparate people in a single imaginary community, and many other countries use them in exactly the same way. American nationalism is unusually intense for a developed country, just as you would expect for a relatively conservative society that escaped serious damage in the nationalist wars of the past century, but it is different from French nationalism or Brazilian nationalism mostly in its intensity, not in its essential character.

When the World Values Survey asked the citizens of fourteen countries if they were "very proud" of their nationality in 1999–2000, no European countries except ultra-nationalist Ireland and Poland reached the 50 per cent mark. Americans ended up at 72 per cent, between the Indians and the Vietnamese. So much for the allegedly greater power of ethnic nationalism – and American nationalism has actually intensified recently. University of Chicago researchers reported that before 9/11, 90 per cent of the Americans surveyed agreed with the statement "I would rather be a citizen of America than of any other country in the world"; afterwards, 97 per cent agreed.

Yet most Americans honestly do not recognize that they are nationalists like everybody else, living in a country with a highly nationalistic foreign policy. When attacked, as they were on 9/11, they interpret it as an assault not on their foreign policy but on their ideals. "They hate our freedoms," says President Bush, as if Osama bin Laden gave a damn one way or the other about the political principles by which Americans run their own affairs. The particular character of American nationalism makes it easier for an administration to mislead people about "why they hate us."

It also makes it easier to lead Americans into crusades abroad on false pretences, at least in the short run. In the United States, the explanation that a foreign adventure will bring the lucky recipient "American values" carries considerable weight, since most Americans believe that their values are superior to those of other peoples. Indeed, they generally believe that other peoples have little chance of achieving democracy without the example and perhaps even the direct help of the United States, which is therefore the chief moral actor in the current era of world history. This belief can occasionally be a constraint on the US government's freedom of action, since it demands that every American use of force abroad have a moral justification, but speech writers usually bridge that gap without too much difficulty. On balance, it may even be easier for the US government to use force, since there is a popular assumption that America *only* uses force for moral reasons.

"The US cannot spread its liberalism without military power as well ... We're talking about the US serving as an organizing principle for the gradual expansion of civil society around the world, and making moral statements simply is not enough to spur that expansion. You also need military power, and you have to periodically show that you are willing to use it."

– Robert D. Kaplan, *Atlantic Monthly*, June 2003

The United States was the first mass society ever to carry out a democratic revolution, which is an imperishable achievement: to a large extent, Americans invented the methods by which a society of equals can become self-governing. But that was more than two hundred years ago, and in the wider world the examples of the French Revolution (which raised issues of racial, class, and gender equality largely ignored by the American Revolution) and of the slowly evolving British model of parliamentary democracy have been just as influential in shaping the many dozens of democratic societies that exist today. In the past twenty years, non-Western societies of many different cultural backgrounds have demonstrated both their desire for democracy and their ability to seize it from corrupt and oppressive rulers by non-violent means, as have European countries living under totalitarian regimes. None of this is acknowledged in the largely self-referential American debate, however, and so it sounds perfectly plausible (within the United States) to argue that America must go to war "to make the world safe for democracy." It allowed President Woodrow Wilson to sell a plain, old-fashioned imperial war to Americans as a crusade for freedom in 1917, and it let President George W. Bush do exactly the same thing in 2003.

This brings us to the next question: Was George W. Bush himself a paid-up neo-conservative, or merely (in the old Leninist jargon) a "useful idiot"? The stock answer is that you have to be interested in ideas before you can be captured by an ideology, so he can't really be a neo-conservative ideologue himself, but that is obviously too simple. He does not seem to be a person who is intellectually engaged, but he is a sufficiently adroit politician to realize that if you do not have an explicit ideological framework yourself, you would be wise to surround yourself with people who do. Before he decided to run for the presidency in 1999, there is no evidence that Bush had any interest in or knowledge of foreign affairs beyond the disdain for alliances and international institutions and the preference for unilateralism that was ingrained in the old, mostly Southern-based Robert Taft wing of the Republican Party, but when he did he surrounded himself with a group of advisers, the so-called Vulcans, whose views were congenial to his own. "Nobody needs to tell me what to believe," as he put it, "but I *do* need somebody to tell me where Kosovo is."

The key members of the Vulcans were Condoleezza Rice and Paul Wolfowitz; others included Robert Blackwill, deputy national security adviser for strategic planning and President Bush's special representative for Iraq until the end of 2004, Richard Perle, and Richard Armitage (deputy secretary of state in George W. Bush's first administration). It appears to have been Rice who shaped the distinctly neo-conservative flavour of this team of advisers – the name is taken from the statue of Vulcan, Roman god of fire, that overlooks her steel-making hometown of Birmingham, Alabama – and the Vulcans, in turn, steered Bush towards his surprise choice of Dick Cheney, neo-conservative *par excellence*, as his vice-presidential running mate. But this does not necessarily lead to a conclusion that he was the victim of an ideological kidnapping.

It is striking that none of the Vulcans had figured prominently among President George H.W. Bush's advisers. From the start, the younger Bush was determined to follow a different course, and while it is pointless to psychologize about how the relationship between the two men may have influenced this outcome, it seems clear that the older man, while maintaining a dignified silence, was not sympathetic to the worldview of the people who surrounded his son. George W. Bush may be a "gut player," as he said, rather than an intellectual neo-conservative, but he was definitely a fully committed member of the team.

Another question that is often raised is about the unusually high proportion of Zionists with close links to the Likud Party in Israel among the ranks of the neo-conservatives. Granted that there was a general consensus in the Bush administration on the desirability of resurrecting *Pax Americana*, how much was the obsessive focus on Iraq driven by the priorities of these Likudniks?

Just mentioning that a significant number of the leading neo-conservatives are Jewish Americans who have close connections with the Israeli government will bring accusations of anti-Semitism, but that is an inevitable cost of commenting on Israeli–American relations and must simply be borne. The Israeli tail succeeds in wagging the US foreign-policy dog quite often – indeed, the last American president to defy Israel openly was George Bush Sr., who forced the Israeli government to attend the Madrid conference on a Middle Eastern peace in fulfilment of his promises to America's Arab allies in the 1990–91 Gulf War, and he is convinced that he paid a high electoral price for it – but that is a normal part of politics. Israel enjoys strong sentimental support among American voters, and all Israeli governments work hard to perpetuate the popular American belief that Israel is a vital US strategic asset in the Middle East. The real question is whether this powerful Israeli influence has been shaping American foreign policy in ways that serve Israeli interests to the detriment of American interests.

The leading Jewish members of the neo-conservative group, like Wolfowitz, Perle, Feith, and Abrams, were not just Zionists, a nationalist movement that commands the loyalty of most but certainly not all Jews. They were Likudniks, closely tied to the ultra-nationalist right-wing party that first came to power in Israel under Menachem Begin in 1977 and regained power under Ariel Sharon in 2001, and it may be presumed that they largely shared Sharon's vision of an Israel permanently in possession of much of the occupied West Bank and permanently superior militarily (in alliance with the United States) to all of its Arab neighbours. Destroying the Baathist regime in Iraq was certainly part of that vision, but it seems to have had an equal appeal to the larger number of non-Jewish ultra-nationalists who make up the small core group of neo-conservatives. None of them saw any contradiction between the Likud's vision for Israel within the Middle East region and their own larger vision for America's strategic future.

Did George W. Bush's own evangelical faith shape his strategic vision, especially in the Middle East? He undoubtedly has a sense of divine mission. Stephen Mansfield recounts in his book *The Faith of George W. Bush* that the then-presidential hopeful told a Texas evangelist at the end of the 1990s: "I feel like God wants me to run for President. I can't explain it, but I sense my country is going to need me. Something is going to happen – I know it won't be easy on me or my family, but God wants me to do it." However, there is no evidence that the general atmosphere of religious fervour that characterized the Bush White House from the start directly translated into US strategy in the Middle East. The fundamentalist Christian religious influence on US foreign policy came much more from the Republican grassroots.

Although American voters are not generally swayed by foreign issues, the future of Israel and of the Middle East is of great interest to one large voting bloc: those among the born-again Christians who subscribe to the belief that we are living in the End Times, and who insist that the United States support the most extreme expansionists in Israel because they actively look forward to a great war in the Middle East. They hope not to have to experience that war themselves, since they expect to be swept up to heaven in the Rapture, but the forces of the anti-Christ – the leading suspects for this role are the United Nations, the Muslim world, the "axis of evil," or the European Union – will ravage the world during the seven years of the Tribulation until they are defeated in a great final battle with the forces of goodness in the valley of Armageddon, in northern Israel. At this point, just before the Messiah returns to walk the earth for a thousand years, all the world's Jews will either convert to Christianity or be destroyed, but at earlier points in the script the Israelis are needed to fulfil the prophecies: they must conquer the rest of the "Biblical lands" (most of the Middle East) and build the Third Temple on the site in Jerusalem now occupied by the al-Aqsa Mosque. And the United States must help them to accomplish these goals.

An estimated 15 to 18 per cent of American voters belong to churches or movements that follow these teachings, and since it would be virtually unthinkable for them to vote Democratic, they may make up as much as a third of the country's potential Republican voters. When President Bush had the temerity to ask Prime Minister Sharon to withdraw his tanks from the West Bank city of Jenin in 2002, he reportedly received a hundred thousand angry e-mails from Americans who believe these prophecies, and he never mentioned the matter again.

In the view of the End-Timers, it is their Christian duty to help realize the prophecies that will bring on the Rapture, the Tribulation, and the thousand-year reign of Christ on the earth by supporting the expansion of Israel and the expulsion of the Palestinians from the land God gave to the Jews – and they must not slow history down by working for peace. As tele-evangelist Jim Robison said when delivering the opening prayer at a Republican National Convention: "There will be no peace until Jesus comes. Any preaching of peace prior to this return is heresy. It is against the word of God. It is anti-Christ." Moreover, the believers do specifically see the US invasion of Iraq as part of the necessary preliminaries to the unleashing of the final war, since Revelations 9: 14–15 speaks of four angels "which are bound in the great river Euphrates" who will be set free "to slay the third part of men." Somewhere near Fallujah, no doubt.

The fervent desire of this key group of Republican voters for a greatly expanded Israel was not easy to reconcile with the Bush administration's formal position of support for a "two-state solution" in Israel/Palestine, but it was only verbal support and no more to be taken seriously than Ariel Sharon's lip service to the same ideal. The End-Timers had little to complain about in the actual actions of the Bush administration in the Middle East in 2001–04. Only one senior cabinet officer in the first Bush administration, Attorney General John Ashcroft, was closely associated with the End-Timers; their influence on policy came more from their huge importance to the Republican Party at election time. But when you combine that outside influence with the less extreme but still devout fundamentalist Protestant majority and the Likudnik Zionist minority in the administration itself, the forces that drove the Bush administration's policies in the Middle East become more comprehensible. There was no Zionist or end-timer plot, but the religious beliefs, strategic perspectives and electoral concerns that dominated the administration provided ample opportunities for Israel to influence American foreign policy. Did the Israel government exploit this situation? Of course it did, but how could it resist?

The attacks on the World Trade Center and the Pentagon on September 11, 2001, created a psychological atmosphere in which America was allegedly at war and the constitutional rules were unofficially suspended. The neo-conservatives' hesitancy about cooking the intelligence on Iraq vanished, and at the same time selling an attack on Iraq got a lot easier, for after 9/11 almost anything they wanted to do on their real agenda could be marketed as part of the "war on terror." The terrorist attacks were a godsend for the neo-conservatives – but first they had to deal with the awkward fact that the attacks had actually been planned in Afghanistan.

It grows clearer each month, as bits of evidence trickle out, that the invasion of Iraq moved from its previous position high on the neo-conservative wish list into the realm of seriously planned operations as soon as the 9/11 attacks made it a politically saleable proposition, and various preparations were set in motion. "We won't do Iraq now," Bush told Condoleezza Rice on September 16, 2001 (as reported in Bob Woodward's book *Bush at War*). "We're putting Iraq off. But eventually we'll have to return to that question." Former CIA director James Woolsey was sent off on a private mission to find any shred of intelligence linking Saddam Hussein to al-Qaeda (he came up blank), a steady drip-feed of administration leaks about Saddam's dangerous weapons of mass destruction began to flow to the media, and on November 21 Bush called in Donald Rumsfeld and told him, "Let's get started on this," ordering him to begin secretly updating the military's plans for an attack on Iraq. But politically it was an absolute priority to deal with Afghanistan first.

The US invasion of Afghanistan was in no way related to the neo-conservative strategy, and could not be made to serve it. What the neo-conservatives wanted to do was to make a deliberate and unprovoked attack on an uncooperative regime and send a message to the world that the United States was now running things; invading Afghanistan would be simply a US response to a flagrant aggression that sent no message other than "Don't attack the United States." But Afghanistan could not be ignored. It was where the al-Qaeda training camps were, where the 9/11 attacks had been planned, where Osama bin Laden himself was. American public opinion quite reasonably wanted that threat dealt with as soon as possible, and the Bush administration had to comply. If Al Gore had been president in Bush's place, *he* would have had to order the invasion of Afghanistan after 9/11.

One of the hallmarks of a good strategy is that it actually compels your opponent to do your will, and in that sense al-Qaeda's strategy for 9/11 was sound: the Bush administration was compelled to invade Afghanistan. The way that it went about it, however, confounded bin Laden's likely expectation, based on his experience of the long guerrilla war against the Soviet army in Afghanistan in the 1980s, that he and his Taliban allies could entangle the invading American troops in another long and costly war. On the contrary, the planning and conduct of the US invasion of Afghanistan was a model of how to do a difficult military operation with maximum speed and minimum casualties.

Getting into Afghanistan has never been that hard: a roll-call of invaders from Alexander the Great to nineteenth-century Britons and twentieth-century Soviets have managed it without too much trouble. The difficulty is in staying there: managing the fractious and xenophobic tribes, controlling the hills that overlook the roads, and dealing with the harsh climate, the scarcity of resources, and the sheer inaccessibility of most of the country. Foreseeing that the

American strategists planning the invasion would try to enlist the support of the ethnic militias of northern Afghanistan, which had lost the 1991–96 civil war and now clung to some strips of territory up on the former Soviet border, Osama bin Laden arranged for the suicide-bombing assassination of the Northern Alliance's charismatic leader, Ahmed Shah Masood, in his Panjshir valley headquarters only two days before al-Qaeda's teams of suicide-hijackers hit New York and Washington.

The US planners did aim for an alliance with the northern militias just as bin Laden foresaw, but their strategy was much bolder and less conventional than he expected. They decided to skip a ground invasion altogether. Instead, they combined the Northern Alliance's numerous but poorly trained troops, CIA and Special Forces teams on the ground, and the US Air Force's precision-guided weapons and unmanned aerial reconnaissance vehicles in a strategy designed to break the Taliban's power quickly and without significant American casualties. It was just the sort of situation where Donald Rumsfeld's cherished "revolution in military affairs" doctrine could be deployed to maximum advantage, and he imposed it unhesitatingly on a doubtful army high command.

Sympathetic offers of military aid flooded in from America's friends and allies, including all the countries that would shun the illegal invasion of Iraq sixteen months later – Canada, France, Germany, Russia – although only a favoured few countries were invited to contribute forces to the combat phase of the operation. The Taliban rulers were formally asked by the US State Department to hand over bin Laden and the other al-Qaeda leaders and to dismantle the terrorist training camps on Afghan soil, although it warned them that there would be no second chance if they became evasive and tried to haggle (as they predictably did). The UN Security Council did not explicitly authorize the invasion of Afghanistan, but its resolutions of September 12 and 28 implicitly gave permission for the US attack, although the situation did not precisely fit the UN Charter rule that grants countries the right of self-defence, and so great was sympathy for the United States that no member of the Security Council sought to oppose the American invasion.

Pakistan and Russia were very helpful in providing supply bases and overflight rights, and in persuading the various Central Asian "Stans" north of Afghanistan to do the same. CIA teams with suitcases full of money and communications equipment made the deals with the various Tajik, Turkmen, Hazara, and Uzbek militias that held the northern fifth of Afghanistan and began to buy up various Taliban commanders. They were soon joined by Special Forces teams with target-designator equipment to guide American bombs very precisely onto the Taliban forces facing the Northern Alliance. By the time the first US and British weapons fell on Afghanistan on October 7, legal and diplomatic niceties had been observed and the vast majority of the world's nations had offered their support or at least their good wishes for the US military operation.

A month later massive US bombing cracked the Taliban lines open. When Kabul fell on November 13, there were still fewer than five hundred Americans on the ground in Afghanistan. With the capture of Mullah Omar's headquarters in the southwestern city of Kandahar on December 7, the war was effectively over: only two months from beginning to end. By then most of al-Qaeda's camps had already been bombed to rubble, most of the "Arab Afghan" fighters still in Afghanistan had been killed or captured, and bin Laden was on the run. Afghan civilian casualties had been lower than even the most optimistic estimates, because for the most part the bombing had not involved urban areas. It was a nearly flawless military operation.

What should have happened next was a flood of foreign soldiers and civilians pouring into Afghanistan, most of them under the UN flag, accompanied by ample supplies and money. Their jobs would have been to scour the countryside for fugitive Taliban and al-Qaeda leaders, bring the victorious northern warlords under control, build a democratic central government and a national army, feed and clothe the desperate rural population, bring the millions of refugees back, and rebuild the country's shattered infrastructure. In other words, eliminate al-Qaeda, de-Talibanize the country, and put it on the road to a more hopeful future. As for the US military, any troops that were not needed in Afghanistan should have been sent home, because there were no more actual battles to fight in the "war on terror." Afghanistan was the only place where the Islamist terrorists had had real bases and the protection of a sovereign government. Elsewhere, they were just civilians living among other civilians, and an army was an entirely inappropriate instrument for chasing them down.

But none of this happened. Throughout 2002–03, almost all of the United Nations troops were confined to Kabul and its immediate neighbourhood, while the US military retained control over the rest of the country in order to hunt the remnants of al-Qaeda and the Taliban down. Because the United States was reluctant to commit a large number of ground troops to Afghanistan, however, the physical control of rural areas was entrusted for the most part to the local warlords. The result was that, while a certain degree of security and normality was restored in the capital, the interim government under Mohammed Karzai that was installed under American auspices in December 2001 never succeeded in establishing its authority over the provinces, where the warlords and their militias retained control. Even Osama bin Laden's apparent escape during the battle of the Tora Bora mountains east of Jalalabad in late December 2001 was at least partly due to the fact that the US command did not commit American troops to the fight, leaving it to Afghan militias and Pakistani border troops, some of whom were allegedly bribed to allow bin Laden to escape across the border.

It was only in late 2003 that the United States began to "encourage" (i.e., allow) the UN troops to move out into the provinces, but by then the window of opportunity had all but closed: the local militias were firmly in control in the plains and valleys, the Taliban were making a comeback in the hills, the opium industry (largely suppressed by the Taliban) was once again the world's biggest, providing much of the rural income, and the so-called national government was a despised shadow with little authority beyond Kabul city limits. Chronic insecurity had led to foreign and even local development agencies withdrawing from many rural areas (where girls were still largely excluded from schools). How did it all go so wrong so fast?

Part of the reason was a US reluctance to commit American troops to combat in Afghanistan. The US army was well aware of the country's reputation as a place where military occupations always failed in the end, most recently in the case of the Soviet occupation, so senior army officers wanted to keep American troops out of combat: that way they wouldn't alienate the locals so much, and they'd keep their own casualties down. At the same time, however, they very much wanted to hunt down the remnants of the Taliban and al-Qaeda, and they didn't trust the troops of other countries, operating under the UN flag, to do that job properly. That left only the local militias – which meant that the warlords had to be left in charge of their local areas, which in turn meant no effective central government, no rural security, not much of anything to show for the American occupation. Add in the neo-conservative mantra about how the United States "doesn't do nation-building," and you have most of the answer. But there was one more thing: a lot of the American troops who might have gone to Afghanistan to help stabilize the place were being held back in readiness for the next war, and most of the political attention in Washington had already moved there.

"The mission begins in Baghdad, but it does not end there. We stand at the cusp of a new historical era. It is so clearly about more than Iraq. It is about more even than the future of the Middle East. It is about what sort of role the United States intends to play in the twenty-first century."

– William Kristol and Lawrence Kaplan, *War over Iraq:*
Saddam's Tyranny and America's Mission (2003)

"We're going to be on the ground in Iraq, as soldiers and citizens, for years. We're going to be running a colony almost."

– Paul Bremer, to a business audience, early March 2004

Once Afghanistan was out of the way, the administration acted fast to move its real agenda into the public domain, carefully painted to resemble the "war on terror." In late December, chief White House speech writer Michael Gerson asked David Frum, a member of his team, to sum up in a sentence or two the best case for going after Iraq. It was a tough assignment, because there was no real link between Saddam Hussein and the Islamist terrorists who had attacked America and obviously he couldn't mention *Pax Americana*, but after working at the problem for a few days Frum came up with the phrase "axis of hatred." It was meant to evoke shadowy ties between all those people who allegedly hated America, and specifically between Iraq and al-Qaeda.

It was nonsense, of course. Even if Saddam Hussein did hate the United States, he could not possibly co-operate with Osama bin Laden. Saddam was a secular dictator, leader of the pan-Arab nationalist and socialist Baath Party, and an accomplished killer and torturer of Islamist radicals, whom he rightly saw as a threat to his regime. Bin Laden was an Islamist zealot who preached the overthrow of secular rulers, the suppression of Arab nationalism and other national identities among Muslims in favour of a single borderless Muslim loyalty, and quite specifically the destruction of the Baath Party and of Saddam Hussein. But not two Americans in a hundred understood enough about Arab and Muslim politics to realize that the two men could not conceivably work together, so Frum's phrase would sound good enough to sway the public. Gerson bought Frum's suggestion, pausing only to change it to "axis of evil" on the grounds that Americans prefer a more theological turn of phrase, and passed it up the line to the policymakers who were working on President Bush's State of the Union message. There were anti-regime riots occurring in Iran as the speech was being written, so Condoleezza Rice suggested adding Iran to the list to encourage the rioters. Then, in order to keep it from looking like an anti-Muslim crusade, North Korea was added to the list for "balance." By the time the speech went out on January 29, 2002, the "axis of evil" included the entire front rank of the neo-conservative hit list.

They were packaged in a different way, however. Now it was the allegation that these three countries were working on or already possessed weapons of mass destruction that put them in the front rank – that, and the suggestion that they were ruled by madmen consumed by hatred of America who would readily give those weapons to terrorists to use against the United States. In the real world, none of these states had been involved with any terrorists targeting the United States for at least the previous ten years, and the idea that any of them would hand over their precious nuclear weapons (if they had any) to Osama bin Laden's Islamist fanatics was simply ridiculous. But this speech was directed at Bush's badly frightened domestic audience, still reeling from 9/11 and many subsequent terrorist scares, and it worked just fine with them.

Few of them, for example, would have realized how odd it was that, while North Korea claimed to have a few working nuclear weapons and Iran was accused of having a nuclear weapons programme, it was Iraq, whose programme had been comprehensively dismantled by UN arms inspectors after the 1990–91 Gulf War, that was Bush's main target. Iraq got five sentences in the speech, versus one each for Iran and North Korea. "States like these, and their terrorist allies, constitute an axis of evil arming to threaten the peace of the world," Bush told his 52 million viewers. "By seeking weapons of mass destruction, these regimes pose a grave and growing danger. They could provide these weapons to terrorists, giving them the means to match their hatred … Time is not on our side. I will not wait on events, while dangers gather. I will not stand by, as peril draws closer and closer. The United States of America will not permit the world's most dangerous regimes to threaten us with the world's most dangerous weapons … History has called America and our allies to action, and it is both our responsibility and our privilege to fight freedom's fight."

It was a paranoid masterpiece, with hardly a single verifiable fact in it, but what was new was the stark unilateralism and rejection of international law implicit in the promise that the United States would attack these countries as and when it chose. With this speech, the public focus of the Bush administration abruptly shifted from terrorists to recalcitrant countries that defied the United States, and the idea that the United States must act alone and above the law was suddenly presented as a necessary response to the "threat" from these states and their alleged terrorist friends. By the most amazing coincidence, the long-term US response to 9/11, now that Afghanistan had been taken care of, turned out to require precisely the policies that the neo-conservatives had been advocating for years as the necessary preconditions for putting *Pax Americana* on a sustainable basis.

To put the question plainly: Did the neo-conservatives in the administration deliberately and consciously hijack the national panic over the 9/11 terrorist attacks in order to impose their own quite different agenda on US foreign policy, starting with the invasion of Iraq? And while we're at it, we should also deal with the mother of all conspiracy theories, which holds that 9/11 was so useful to the neo-conservatives who dominated the Bush administration that they must have either (a) planned it or (b) deliberately ignored prior intelligence about it.

Version (a) is popular mainly among Arabs and other Muslims who want to deny any Arab or Muslim role in the events at all, and blame it instead on a conspiracy between the CIA and the Israelis. It is frequently buttressed by the outright lie, now treated by most people in the Arab world as established fact, that Jews working in the Twin Towers were warned not to go to work on the morning of September 11. (Jews were, of course, fully and proportionally represented among the victims of 9/11.) This conspiracy theory is unworthy of further consideration – but the other version has to be treated more seriously.

The idea that at least some people in the Bush administration had intelligence forewarning of the al-Qaeda attack, but chose not to act on it, is a myth that will eventually take its place alongside the conspiracy theories about the Kennedy assassination in the collective American subconscious. But conspiracies do happen from time to time, and they may even have happened in Washington from time to time, so what are the grounds for dismissing this conspiracy theory out of hand? After all, it is now generally accepted that at least some bits of information pointing to the 9/11 hijackers were floating around in the US intelligence world. How come somebody didn't put them together and stop the attack?

This whole theory rests on a profound misunderstanding of the way intelligence gathering works. The conspiracy theorists imagine a single vital piece of intelligence that reveals the plot, rather than the reality of a stream of raw data flowing across analysts' desks, some of it reliable, some questionable, and some of it plausible but wrong, in which the analysts try to see patterns and connections that may reveal what is actually going on. Sometimes they spot genuine patterns and get it right, but they also get a lot of false positives, and they often miss patterns that really exist. It's like playing Connect the Dots with all but a few of the data points missing, and quite a few false ones scattered around for good measure. Stuff gets missed that a luckier guess might have discerned – and after the disaster happens, you can always go back into the old data stream, pick out the data points that should have been joined up, and hang the analysts for negligence. In other words, the fact that some relevant bits of good intelligence were floating around in the system did *not* mean that good analysts were bound to come to the right conclusion.

But let us suppose that some low-level analyst did realize what was coming and urgently passed the intelligence up the chain to the head of the CIA or the FBI. How many people would know by then that this vital information had been received? At least half a dozen, for the raw intelligence data passes through several levels before it reaches the director's desk. How could they all be silenced – and how many more people at the decision-making level would have to be brought into the picture before a decision could be made just to sit on the intelligence and do nothing? Half a dozen more, at the very least. What chance is there that a conspiracy involving so many people from many different backgrounds would remain secret for long? Approximately zero. What would be the penalty for deliberately ignoring such a warning in order to further a partisan agenda? The crimes involved are high treason and accessory to mass murder, and the penalty is death. What is the likelihood that any senior official, knowing all this, would propose a conspiracy to suppress the intelligence and just let 9/11 happen? Absolutely zero.

Once 9/11 actually happened, how many neo-conservatives high in the Bush administration deliberately used the panic as a way of advancing their own project? That is a quite different question, for an ability to seize upon passing events and use them to support your own agenda is a highly valued skill among Washington's bureaucratic warriors. The strategy of bait-and-switch is the same whether you're selling cars or political policies, and nobody in the neo-conservative circle would have seen it as illegitimate. The more sensitive souls among them probably preferred to avoid too close an examination of the way the sale was being made, but that's how politics works all around the world. If your motives are good and your policy is sound, in the view of most practitioners, then a little bit of legerdemain with the actual arguments is no crime.

The key thing about Bush's State of the Union speech, reiterated and amplified by public statements made by senior neo-conservative members of the administration over the following weeks and months, was the "new doctrine called pre-emption," as the president later referred to it. But it wasn't really about pre-emptive war, where a country facing an imminent and obvious intention to attack on the part of an enemy may, under strictly defined circumstances, act first to blunt that attack. Pre-emptive war is what Israel did to the Arab states in 1967, and it is sometimes legal under traditional international law.

"America will act against ... emerging threats before they are fully formed," Bush wrote in the introduction to the annual *National Security Strategy* document. "We will not hesitate to act alone, if necessary ... The greater the threat, the greater is the risk of inaction – and the more compelling the case for taking anticipatory action to defend ourselves, even if uncertainty remains as to the time and place of the enemy's attack." That is not pre-emptive war; it is *preventive* war, where you attack a country because you think it might attack you or become more dangerous to you at some future time. It is never legal, but it is the doctrine that the neo-conservatives wanted and needed.

The administration's cheerleaders in the US media were ecstatic about the State of the Union message. Charles Krauthammer of the

Washington Post rhapsodized that "Iraq is what this speech was about … The speech was just short of a declaration of war." America's friends and allies abroad understood that too, but were shocked and confused by the sudden swerve of US policy away from the war on terrorism and towards an illegal and seemingly irrational war of aggression against Iraq. British foreign secretary Jack Straw tried to pass it off as a momentary aberration driven by domestic political considerations and "best understood by the fact that there are mid-term congressional elections coming up in November." Canada's foreign minister, Bill Graham, simply sounded puzzled: "Nobody is supporting Saddam Hussein, but everyone recognizes in international politics you have to have a process where, before you invade a sovereign state, there has to be a reason for it, or we are going to have international chaos." They doubtless knew who the neo-conservatives were, but they still hadn't grasped the fact that they ran the place.

They did run the place, and a few months after Bush's January speech Randy Beers, a former Foreign Service officer who had served in the White House in various intelligence, counter-terrorism, and foreign military policy roles under four presidents (three of them Republicans), stopped by Dick Clarke's house in Washington for some advice. Beers had ended up in more or less the same National Security Council job that Clarke had left in frustration only a month after 9/11, co-ordinating counter-terrorism activities – but as Clarke tells it in *Against All Enemies*, Beers was now thinking of quitting too. Clarke opened some wine, and Beers spilled his guts.

"They still don't get it. Insteada goin' all out against al Qaeda and eliminating our vulnerabilities at home, they wanna fuckin' invade Iraq again," he told his old friend. The United States still hadn't caught bin Laden or Mullah Omar, the Taliban leader, and the Taliban were regrouping in the hills, but Washington was restricting its military commitment in Afghanistan to a token force and holding back the bulk of available US forces for the invasion of Iraq. "Do you know how much it will strengthen al Qaeda and groups like that if we occupy Iraq?" Beers raged. "There's no threat to us now from Iraq, but 70 per cent of the American people think Iraq attacked the Pentagon and the World Trade Center. You wanna know why? Because that's what the administration wants them to think! … I can't work for these people. I'm sorry, I just can't." So Beers quit too. A year later he volunteered to serve as chief foreign policy adviser for John Kerry's campaign to unseat the Bush presidency.

"Frankly, [sanctions] have worked. [Saddam] has not developed any significant capability with respect to weapons of mass destruction. He is unable to project conventional power against his neighbours."

– US secretary of state Colin Powell, Cairo, February 24, 2001

"When I left the Foreign Office in 2001, we all believed that the strategy of containment was working and was denying Saddam the ability to develop weapons of mass destruction … The development that prompted the switch from containment to invasion was not any new intelligence on Iraq but regime change in Washington … This was a war made in Washington by an administration that chose Iraq not because it really imagined Iraq was a threat, but because it knew the country was weak and could not resist …"

– Robin Cook, former British foreign secretary
(resigned from British cabinet in 2003 over Iraq),
Independent on Sunday, July 18, 2004

No credible new intelligence data about alleged Iraqi WMD came into the hands of the US and British intelligence services between 2001 and the invasion of Iraq in March 2003, so what happened? A huge amount of effort has gone into dissecting the way that intelligence data were misused in the year following Bush's 2002 State of the Union speech, both in the United States and in Britain, in order to produce a convincing case for attacking Iraq. Congressional and parliamentary committees and commissions have sifted the evidence, all agreeing that the flimsy scraps of "intelligence" that were produced to suggest that Saddam Hussein had weapons of mass destruction of some sort and represented a danger to the United States and Britain, and that he was in contact with al-Qaeda and in some way linked to the 9/11 attacks, were false. (Most came from deeply suspect Iraqi exile sources.) But these examinations either left the question of the political responsibility for these falsehoods unanswered until after the next election (in the case of the United States), or concluded that although huge mistakes had been made, no one was to blame (in the case of the United Kingdom). That was hardly surprising, since the inquiries were either appointed (very reluctantly) by the government in power, or dominated by members of that government's party in the legislature. They were useful in terms of keeping the question of the culpability of the two governments on the public agenda, but the details of these inquiries would fill another book – and in any case, they are not necessary to understand what happened.

In the United States, it was a straightforward selling job: come up with reasons that will persuade the American public that it's a good idea to attack Iraq. Given how traumatized most Americans were by the shock of 9/11, and how reluctant they were to question presidential leadership at a time of perceived crisis when patriotism was at fever pitch and solidarity was an obligation, it was not a very difficult task.

"For reasons that have a lot to do with the US government bureaucracy, we settled on the one issue everyone could agree on, which was weapons of mass destruction..."

– Paul Wolfowitz, *Vanity Fair*, June 2003

A certain amount of selective manipulation of intelligence was necessary in order to produce "evidence" for Congress and for international diplomatic purposes (and a secret cell called the Office of Special Plans was set up within Rumsfeld's Pentagon under the control of Doug Feith to mine the intelligence data for nuggets that had been rejected by the normal intelligence process as unreliable, but might help to "prove" the existence of Iraq's WMD and its contacts with al-Qaeda). The main sales job on the American public, however, was done with pure rhetoric. Over a period of a year, in almost every public speech made by President Bush, Vice-President Cheney, and other senior members of the administration, the words *Iraq* or *Saddam Hussein* were mentioned in the same breath as *weapons of mass destruction*, *al-Qaeda*, or *9/11* at least a couple of times. Bush and his colleagues, clearly acting on expert legal advice, were careful never to say explicitly that the Iraqi leader was responsible for 9/11, but their rhetorical campaign was so successful that by the time the invasion actually began in March, 2003, about 70 per cent of Americans believed that Saddam had sent the terrorists.

There was still a residual unease, however, about the fact that almost none of America's traditional allies saw things the same way: they had all volunteered for Afghanistan, but this time most of them weren't coming. The idea of *Pax Americana* was that the United States would make the decisions and other countries would obediently fall in behind, trusting American judgement or fearing American power, but they *were* expected to fall in. It was never the intention that the United States should do all the heavy lifting involved in running the world completely alone – and the American public, accustomed for half a century to seeing the same loyal allies alongside the United States in every crisis, was disoriented and even a bit dismayed by their attitude this time. Other governments could see what the neo-conservatives were up to (as they were intended to), and although diplomatic courtesy prevented them from saying that bluntly, some of them, like the Germans, the French, and the Canadians, were being quite vocal about why they thought an attack on Iraq would be illegal and unnecessary, or at least greatly premature. This caused further unease among Americans, so it became very important for Bush to have America's closest traditional ally, Britain, on board for the attack. That complicated matters considerably.

According to Sir Christopher Meyer, former British ambassador to Washington, President Bush first asked Prime Minister Tony Blair for Britain's support in attacking Iraq at a private dinner in Washington just nine days after the 9/11 attacks, and Blair "said nothing to demur," but his formal (though still secret) commitment to invade Iraq alongside the United States probably only came soon after Bush's key State of the Union speech, likely on Blair's visit to the Crawford ranch in early April 2002. As the time for the invasion approached, however, it became clear that Blair was going to have great difficulty in carrying British popular opinion, and perhaps even the House of Commons, with him. That was the principal reason that less emphasis came to be placed on "regime change" (which was all right with the American audience but was seen as an illegal act of aggression in Britain) and more on the imaginary dangers of Saddam's weapons of mass destruction. "Imaginary dangers," in the sense that even those intelligence services that had deluded themselves into believing that Saddam had WMD didn't think that he had anything except chemical weapons – and chemical weapons are not really weapons of mass destruction in any meaningful sense.

The reason that chemical, biological, and nuclear weapons all ended up in the same category of WMD is that they have all been the target of attempts to impose legal controls or bans on their possession or use – and quite rightly too. But they are not weapons of equal destructiveness. A really big nuclear weapon, exploded in the right place under the right conditions, could kill several million people, and even an average nuclear blast would kill a hundred thousand people or more if detonated in a densely populated area. A chemical warhead is a battlefield weapon, exceedingly nasty but limited in its effect: the worst poison gas attack of recent history, the Iraqi air attack on the town of Halabja in 1988, killed a maximum estimated figure of 6,800 people although it involved aircraft dropping a large number of nerve-gas bombs on the town. A more realistic example of the damage that chemical weapons would do in terrorist hands is provided by the one known case of such an attack, when the Aum Shinrikyo terrorist group released sarin (nerve) gas on a crowded Japanese subway train in 1995. Twelve people died, some dozens were seriously affected, and close to a thousand felt briefly ill. A big nail bomb would probably have killed more people (though it would not have had the same dramatic effect).

It is possible to imagine that the intelligence services of the United States and the United Kingdom believed that Saddam Hussein had secretly kept some chemical weapons despite the seven-year presence of the UN arms inspectors in Iraq in 1991–98. It is not easy to believe that they would have thought this an urgent danger and an adequate reason to invade Iraq. Almost *every* country in the Middle East has chemical weapons: Syria and Egypt certainly do (because Israel does); Iran certainly does (because Iraq used them against it in the 1980–88 war); and Pakistan almost certainly does, because of its confrontation with India. There are tens of thousands of tons of chemical weapons in the Russian Federation, some of them reputedly stored in unguarded depots secured with bicycle locks. Even the United States still had more than 15,000 tons of mustard gas and 13,000 tons of various kinds of nerve gas at the time of its last public accounting of them in 1997.

Even if Iraq also had had a few chemical weapons lying around somewhere, they would not have been a particular threat to anyone who didn't invade Iraq, and terrorists were no more likely to acquire chemical weapons from Iraq than anywhere else. The whole furore over WMD was just a pretext for an invasion that had other purposes and, at a level that will never show up in the reports of the various inquiries, virtually everybody involved in the process on both the intelligence and the governmental side knew it. As Greg Thielmann, then director of the Office of Strategic Proliferation and Military Affairs in the US State Department's Bureau of Intelligence and Research, put it: "Everybody in the intelligence community knew that the White House couldn't care less about any information suggesting that there were no WMDs ..."

Still, it was a necessary fiction, and in an attempt to provide diplomatic and political cover for the British prime minister, Washington and London sought a UN Security Council resolution in November 2002 demanding that arms inspectors be admitted to Iraq to search for Saddam's alleged WMD. They probably assumed that he would refuse, but he did not (he knew he had nothing to hide, after all), which threatened to throw the Anglo-American timetable for an invasion seriously off schedule. The US troop build-up in the region had already begun in the autumn of 2002, and Washington was anxious to get the war over before the extreme heat of summer arrived: the effective deadline to get it started was mid-March.

By February 2003, the major obstacle to an invasion was that the UN arms inspectors in Iraq, who were getting unimpeded access to any sites they wanted, were following up every tip that Western intelligence services deigned to give them – and were finding nothing. This was perplexing to chief UN arms inspector Hans Blix, a hawkish figure who was convinced that Saddam Hussein *was* hiding WMD when he was called out of retirement to lead the Iraq mission. As all the leads confidently provided by US and British intelligence ran into the sand, however, he began to talk privately about "faith-based intelligence gathering" and to suspect that the WMD did not actually exist. As he noted in his memoir, *Disarming*

Iraq: The Search for Weapons of Mass Destruction, "It occurred to me [on March 7] that the Iraqis would be in greater difficulty if … there truly were no weapons of which they could 'yield possession.'"

Tony Blair had promised parliament that he would seek a second UN resolution specifically authorizing an invasion before he joined an attack on Iraq, but it was very unlikely that the majority of the Security Council members would pass such a resolution unless the inspectors reported that they were being hindered by the Iraqis in their work. Indeed, there was a growing danger that, given enough time, the inspectors would report that there were no forbidden weapons in Iraq, thus removing Blair's entire case for joining Bush's war. So he resorted to scare tactics.

"Fish mongers sell fish, war mongers sell war, and both may sincerely believe in their product. But I think the overselling came … in the spring [of 2003], when it looked as though the British people were not actually going to sign up to this project … [T]he continual assessments of an imminent terrorist attack on London, advising housewives to lay in stocks of water and food, I mean all that stuff … tanks at Heathrow. I mean, I call that overselling."

– Sir Rodrick Braithwaite, former head of the [British] joint intelligence committee, *The Guardian*, July 14, 2003

"… [T]he intention was to dramatize it, just as the vendors of some merchandise … exaggerate the importance of what they have. But from politicians, of our leaders, in the Western world, I think we expect a bit more than that – a bit more sincerity."

– Hans Blix, on BBC's *Breakfast with Frost*, February 8, 2004

Why did Tony Blair commit Britain to this adventure at America's side? The professionals in the Foreign Office would probably have advised him to support it, simply because they generally put preserving the "special relationship" with the United

States above all other considerations, but he was under no obligation to accept their advice. There was certainly no appetite for it in Britain, and there could be no personal or party political advantage in it for him: his own Labour Party was acutely uncomfortable at his closeness to the most right-wing American president in living memory, and Labour supporters were even more opposed to the idea of a war with Iraq than other British voters. We are left with only personal explanations for his extraordinary choice.

One was undoubtedly his religious fervour: Tony Blair was probably the most enthusiastic Christian to become prime minister since William Ewart Gladstone left Number 10 for the last time in 1894. (Only 16 per cent of Britons say religion is very important in their lives, compared to 53 per cent of Americans.) One of the highlights of the 2003 television year in Britain was an interview of Blair conducted by Jeremy Paxman, the attack-dog of British TV interviewers, who asked the prime minister if, on his visits to the White House, he prayed with President Bush. Blair affected outrage at the question – a necessary response, given the allergic reaction of the British to displays of religiosity in public life – but he did not say no. While there was a doctrinal and stylistic gulf between the born-again fundamentalists who made up a large share of the White House's population and Blair's orthodox, mainstream Christianity, he shared with them a missionary enthusiasm and an unshakable confidence in the moral rightness of his actions.

As Gladstone had gone out into the streets of Victorian London, picked up fallen women, and brought them home to read the New Testament to them (whipping himself in private afterwards), Tony Blair had acquired the habit of going out into the world and rescuing fallen countries (though his views on self-flagellation are unknown). His principal experience of foreign affairs before Iraq had been three foreign military interventions – in Kosovo in 1999, in Sierra Leone in 2000, and in Afghanistan in 2001 – that had not cost many British lives, that were more or less legal, and that were arguably all on balance beneficial to the people of those countries. So it had been flowers, champagne, and a warm glow of moral righteousness three times for Tony, and he was not averse to more of the same. "I am truly committed to dealing with [Iraq], irrespective of the position of America," he told a *Guardian* interviewer on March 1, 2003. "If the Americans were not doing this, I would be pressuring for them to be doing so." And he told cabinet colleague Clare Short: "If it were down to me, I'd do [invade] Zimbabwe as well."

But how did Blair fail to notice that the Bush administration's motives for invading Iraq were utterly different from his own, and that this was a completely illegal enterprise? Sheer inexperience may be part of the answer: he had never held any government office before he became prime minister in 1997 (the Conservatives had been in power since 1979), but nevertheless often acts as his own foreign minister. It is questionable whether Blair spotted the critical distinction between the previous interventions and Iraq when George W. Bush first asked him to help in the invasion, probably at a time when there were no Foreign Office minders in attendance. At any rate, he said yes – and it is ten times harder to take back your given word than to say no in the first place. It's a poor reason to take a country to war, but when all Blair's other justifications crumbled, he was still able to take refuge in his conviction that overthrowing Saddam Hussein was a morally righteous act.

So it may have been, but it was not a legal act, nor necessarily a wise one, and by late February 2003 it was clear that only a small minority on the UN Security Council would vote in favour of withdrawing the inspectors from Iraq and authorizing an invasion. No banned weapons were being found in Iraq, there was no reason to rush into war, and President Bush's fulminations about Saddam Hussein's policy of "delay and deceit" were sounding increasingly hollow.

Indeed the United States was receiving increasingly desperate peace offers from Saddam Hussein's regime by multiple private routes, including approaches to Richard Perle and to Vincent Cannistraro, the CIA's former head of counter-terrorism, proposing to let several thousand US troops and/or FBI agents into the country to search for the alleged WMD, to grant the United States rights over Iraqi oil, and even to hold internationally monitored elections within two years. But the CIA instructed Perle to reply, "Tell them we will see them in Baghdad," and Cannistraro got a similar response: "There were serious attempts to cut a deal, but they were all turned down by the president and vice-president." Nobody else on the Security Council was told about the approaches, but they were nevertheless deeply suspicious about the Anglo-American attempt to rush the UN into war without hearing the inspectors' report.

"We will not allow the passage of a planned resolution that would authorize the use of force. Russia and France, as permanent Security Council members, will fully assume all their responsibilities on this point. We are totally on the same line on this as the Russians."

– Dominique de Villepin, French foreign minister, March 5, 2003

It wasn't just France. De Villepin had met with his German and Russian colleagues in Paris – what Condoleezza Rice called the "non-nein-nyet" alliance – before issuing his statement. France was prepared to use its veto if necessary, but so was Russia: Alexander Konovalov, president of the Institute for Strategic Studies in Moscow, explained on March 5 that "this is a very strong signal to the United States not to put the second resolution up for a vote at all. After such strong statements, Russia [has to use] its veto if it does come to a vote." Russian foreign minister Igor Ivanov let it be known that China, which also had a veto, "shared the approach" of Paris and

Moscow in opposing a premature resort to force. And Germany, which had a temporary seat on the Security Council but no veto, was equally adamant, Foreign Minister Joschka Fischer saying, "I don't see personally how we can stop the process of Resolution 1441 [which sent the weapons inspectors into Iraq] and resort to war." The results of the inspections, he observed, were "more and more encouraging."

In fact, opposition to war against Iraq was overwhelming on the Security Council. Despite an intense campaign of pressure by the United States and Britain, almost none of the non-permanent members had been persuaded that war was desirable, and the resolution was unlikely to get more than four votes out of fifteen (the United States, Britain, Spain, and perhaps one other). A veto would not be needed. A few weeks earlier, the Anglo-American allies had sworn publicly to force a Security Council vote on the issue, but faced with this united front they withdrew their resolution, falsely claiming that France would block any attempt to use force against Iraq. (France had actually said that it would veto any measure proposing to withdraw the arms inspectors and invade Iraq without completing the process and hearing their report.)

Having abandoned the UN, the United States and Britain declared that they would attack Iraq as soon as the UN inspectors were pulled out. They claimed that Saddam Hussein was obstructing the inspectors and was therefore in breach of Resolution 1441 (something that neither the inspectors nor the Security Council had said), that Iraq's alleged breach of 1441 automatically cancelled the cease-fire of 1991, and that they were therefore entitled to invade Iraq under the original UN Resolution 678 of 1990 that had authorized the use of force to liberate Kuwait (the same resolution that George H.W. Bush and British prime minister John Major had interpreted at the time as *not* authorizing them to invade Iraq and overthrow Saddam Hussein). Saddam let the inspectors leave unharmed, and the assault began on March 20, 2003.

The Iraqi forces, which had received no new equipment since their catastrophic defeat in the first Gulf War twelve years before, were helpless under the shower of precision-guided munitions that destroyed them before they even saw their enemy. Some Baathists fought bravely, but most Iraqi soldiers showed little desire to die for Saddam Hussein. The kill ratio on the battlefield was close to a hundred Iraqis for every dead soldier of the "coalition forces." The allegedly elite Republican Guards divisions were stupidly committed to battle in the open south of Baghdad, where they were promptly annihilated by American air power. There was not even a last stand in Baghdad, the one place where the Iraqi forces could have slowed an American victory and inflicted serious US casualties by forcing a battle in a large built-up area. Baghdad was left virtually undefended, and fell on April 9. It was a splendid success militarily – and a political disaster.

In the first Gulf War, the US forces that liberated Kuwait were accompanied by contingents from almost every NATO country (including France, Germany, and Canada) and by a number of Arab armies. The entire war was waged under the authority of the United Nations, and most of the countries that did not have troops on the ground, like Russia, nevertheless offered their support in other ways. Even in Afghanistan in 2001, practically every country that mattered offered to help in the invasion, although relatively few of them were compatible enough with US forces in equipment and operational procedures to be allocated an active role in the war by the Pentagon.

But in the invasion of Iraq in 2003 there were no Arab allies, and effectively no NATO allies except Britain – even the Turks had refused to let the US use its bases in the country for the attack. In fact, the Americans and the British were all alone on the front line except for a couple of thousand Australians. (Australian defence policy consists primarily of sending Australian troops to every American war, in the hope that if one day Australia needs to have the favour returned, Americans will feel grateful enough to come and help. If the United States invaded Mars, Australia would send a battalion along.) And, of course, there was no UN authority to make it legal: it was just three English-speaking countries invading an Arabic-speaking country, ostensibly as a public service to the world.

This did not matter to the hard-core neo-conservatives, of course. Their whole purpose was to send a message to the world that the rules had changed, and Iraq would do that job just fine. They didn't mind a bit when the arguments about Iraqi WMD and links between Saddam and al-Qaeda on which they had based their public case for war fell apart, either, although it required some verbal gymnastics from President Bush and Prime Minister Blair.

"The Iraqi regime possesses and produces chemical and biological weapons. It is seeking nuclear weapons. … Facing clear evidence of peril, we cannot wait for the final proof, the smoking gun that could come in the form of a mushroom cloud."

– George W. Bush, October 7 and 8, 2002

"We are asked to accept that, contrary to all intelligence, Saddam decided to destroy those weapons. I say such a claim is palpably absurd."

– Tony Blair, March 18, 2003

"He had the capacity to have a weapon, make a weapon. We thought he had weapons. He could have developed a nuclear weapon over time – I'm not saying tomorrow, but over time."

– George W. Bush, February 8, 2004

"I have to accept that we have not found them and we may not find them. He

[Saddam] may have removed or hidden or even destroyed those weapons."

– Tony Blair, July 6, 2004

The Iraqis almost certainly destroyed all their banned weapons in the summer of 1991, just as they always said they had, although they continued to hide some production and research facilities until the UN arms inspectors tracked them down in the mid-1990s. "I don't think they existed," said David Kay, head of the post-war Iraq survey group tasked with finding the WMD, when he resigned from the position after nine fruitless months of hunting for them in January 2004.

The collapse of the "intelligence" on which they had made their case for war severely damaged public trust in Tony Blair in Britain and in Prime Minister John Howard's government in Australia, the only other country to have joined the United States' invasion of Iraq, but it had significantly less impact in the United States. A survey by the University of Maryland found that as late as April 2004, 57 per cent of those interviewed "believe that before the war Iraq was providing substantial support to al-Qaeda," and 65 per cent believed that "experts" had confirmed that Iraq had WMD. The decline in American popular support for the war in Iraq is more likely to be due to mounting US casualties there.

And meanwhile, the other great powers continue to ponder the message that the United States sent them by invading Iraq. They received the message loud and clear, but apart from Britain they have not come to heel. France, Germany, Russia, and China offered only verbal criticism of the invasion of Iraq, but it is clear that they are reconsidering their options in a fundamental way.

CHAPTER V

THE SYSTEM (SUCH AS IT IS)

*The voice from the telescreen paused. A trumpet call, clear and beautiful,
floated into the stagnant air. The voice continued raspingly:*

*"Attention! Your attention, please! A newsflash has arrived this moment
from the Malabar front. Our forces in South India have won a glorious
victory. I am authorised to say that the action we are now reporting may well
bring the war within measurable distance of its end. Here is the newsflash –"*

*Bad news coming, thought Winston. And sure enough, following a gory
description of the annihilation of a Eurasian army, with stupendous figures
of killed and prisoners, came the announcement that, as of next week, the
chocolate ration would be reduced from thirty grammes to twenty. . . .*

*"Oceania, 'tis for thee" gave way to lighter music. Winston walked over to
the window, keeping his back to the telescreen. The day was still cold and
clear. Somewhere far away a rocket bomb exploded with a dull, reverberating
roar. About twenty or thirty of them a week were falling on London at present.*

– George Orwell, *Nineteen Eighty-Four*

I f we could have a safer, fairer global order through the unilateral exercise of American power, many people in the West (though not elsewhere) would reluctantly accept that solution. After all, the United Nations has not exactly been an unqualified success. But most people suspect that *Pax Americana* won't work, because Americans will not be willing to bear for long the burden of high casualties and high taxes that such a policy involves.

What we risk ending up with instead is a world in which all the old institutions of international governance have been destroyed or gravely undermined by the actions of the neo-conservatives, but the rival American bid to provide world order has crashed and burned. We may end up with nothing, in other words. No working multilateral institutions, little by way of international co-operation, and a world whose geopolitics is loosely modelled on George Orwell's *Nineteen Eighty-Four*.

The world of *Nineteen Eighty-Four* as Orwell depicted it never came to pass, though it seemed plausible enough when he wrote the novel in 1948. The post–Second World War world did begin to divide up into the three perpetually warring blocs he imagined, Eurasia, Eastasia, and Oceania (the Americas plus Britain), but the division remained incomplete. China never became the core of a united Eastasian bloc, and the line between Russian-dominated Eurasia and Oceania ran down the middle of Europe along the NATO–Warsaw Pact frontier, not down the English Channel. More importantly, these blocs did not end up perpetually at war with one another, although there were numerous clashes between Oceania and Eastasia (most significantly in Korea and Vietnam) and a terrifying forty-year nuclear confrontation between Oceania and Eurasia.

Most important of all, Oceania – the West – did not succumb to the totalitarian template that defines all three blocs in Orwell's novel. Stalin's Europe and Mao's China came pretty close to the Orwellian nightmare during the 1950s, but the brief interlude of the McCarthy witch hunt in the United States was the closest approach in the West, and it was not close at all. By the 1970s both the Soviet and the Chinese regimes were retreating from the full totalitarian model, perhaps because such regimented viciousness is hard to sustain over long periods of time. Then came the non-violent revolutions of 1989–91, bringing some kind of democracy to most of the countries of Eurasia and ending the Cold War, the main military confrontation in the world. At the same time, China (Eastasia) relaxed politically and integrated into the emerging global economy without a revolution. Orwell's book became a frightful vision of a future that might have been, but never was.

Why didn't it come to pass? One reason was certainly the existence of nuclear weapons, which made any direct military clash between the blocs insanely dangerous. Orwell just ignored their existence. In *Nineteen Eighty-Four* the three blocs fight endless, ritualistic, deliberately indecisive wars whose purpose is to justify domestic repression everywhere, and only conventional weapons are used: the "rocket bombs" he writes of are not nuclear-tipped ICBMS, but near descendants of the Nazi V-2s that did fall on London in 1944. In the real post-1945 world of widespread nuclear weapons, however, you could not have had twenty to thirty Eurasian (i.e., Russian) "rocket bombs" per week falling on London for very long without escalation to all-out nuclear war.

But the more profound reason that *Nineteen Eighty-Four*

remained a fiction was that the most powerful of the three proto-blocs, the West, would not abandon its clumsy, seemingly inefficient democratic system despite the temptation to mobilize for total war, and flatly refused to embark on any kind of ideological crusade. This was largely due to the wisdom of a generation of American leaders in the early post-war years who coped with the Soviet threat, to the extent that it actually existed, by relying on nuclear deterrence to contain the Soviet Union militarily while subsidizing the reconstruction of democracies in western Europe and Japan. Relations between Oceania and Eastasia superficially seemed closer to the Orwellian model for a while, with Western armies fighting limited (non-nuclear) wars around the borders of China almost continuously from 1950 to 1973, but then the West finally figured out that most of these conflicts were really about national liberation from imperial rule and who gets to rule locally afterwards, and direct involvement by Western armies ceased.

There was also a third reason why Orwell's future did not happen, though it rarely gets the credit it deserves. The structure of international laws and rules that came into being with the creation of the United Nations in 1945, and the powerful idea of a global community that it embodied, helped to stave off a descent into a world of universal violence and repression. Even in the darkest days of the Cold War, the superpowers were able to back away from potentially lethal confrontations without loss of face by deferring to the legal authority of the UN Security Council in matters of war and peace. And even in the deepest pits of repression, democrats like the Czech dissidents of Charter 77 and Daw Aung Sang Suu Kyi in Burma could gain some protection by appealing to the world of law imagined by the UN Charter and the International Convention on Human Rights. The law was broken daily, even hourly, but it made a difference that the oppressors generally felt obliged to deny their misdeeds or cloak them in fake legality rather than simply doing them boldly and openly. Nowhere, not even China in the days of the Cultural Revolution, was as bad as Orwell's world.

Nobody wanted *Nineteen Eighty-Four* to come true, least of all Orwell, and he would have been delighted had he lived long enough to learn that his model of the future had been aborted. But history is full of potential turning points, some of which get taken and some of which do not: the real world turned out so much better than Orwell's terrible vision (if still well short of perfect) because individuals and countries made particular decisions and adopted specific policies at certain times.

It is hard to imagine any realistic outcome that would have matched the awfulness of *Nineteen Eighty-Four*, which is after all a novel, but other decisions and policies would have led to other outcomes in the real world, and some of them would have been extremely grim. Which brings us to the present, for the game is never over. There are decisions being made and policies being adopted right now that, if they stand, will deliver us into a world that is much worse than the present, and a good deal closer to Orwell's fantasy.

"This organization is created to keep you from going to hell. It isn't created to take you to heaven."

– Henry Cabot Lodge Jr., Republican
senator and US delegate to the UN, 1955

"I believe that I made the right decision, but I accept it is a big responsibility," said British prime minister Tony Blair in October 2003, six months after the invasion of Iraq. "You are, and should be held to account for such decisions ... Those who started the war must finish it. The judgement will be made by whether we make life better [in Iraq] or not." That was about all that Blair had left to say at that point, given the total absence of the alleged weapons of mass destruction that were his original pretext for attacking Iraq, and a comparable shift of emphasis in justifications for the war occurred in the United States for the same reason.

But even if the American and British governments genuinely felt the pain of oppressed Iraqis (while remaining strangely numb to the pain of oppressed Burmese, Belarussians, and Burundians), the welfare of the Iraqi people was not an adequate legal justification for the unprovoked invasion of a sovereign country. Even if Iraq were to become a bastion of peace, prosperity, and democracy in the Middle East as a result of the Anglo-American invasion – a highly improbable outcome, on present evidence – the attack would remain an act of aggression contrary to international law.

At this point in the argument, a chorus of "so what?" arises from all those who saw their short-term purposes served by the elimination of Saddam Hussein's regime, and they were quite numerous. Americans and some others who obsessed about terrorism and believed the myths about Iraqi WMD and Saddam's alleged links with al-Qaeda; US neo-conservatives who saw the Iraq War as the opening shot of their campaign to impose *Pax Americana* on the world; Israelis who regarded Iraq as the largest remaining threat to their military hegemony in the region – they all felt that the benefits of an armed invasion of Iraq outweighed the damage to the international rule of law, which is longer-term and less easily comprehended. The humanitarian argument that Iraqis are better off without Saddam Hussein, the fallback justification for the invasion after the alleged WMD evaporated, may turn out to be true in the end – we won't really know for years – but even if that really had been their motive, it wouldn't be enough. The implications of the illegal invasion of Iraq for the international system are huge and entirely negative, and the fallout from that deed may blight our world for many years.

We are not dealing here with the obvious first-order consequences of the invasion, like the guerrilla war in Iraq against the occupation forces, the further alienation of Arab and Muslim countries, and the likely boost that this will give to the phenomenon of international Islamist terrorism. It is the international system itself that is at risk, for when the United States and Great Britain, both permanent members of the UN Security Council, invaded Iraq in the teeth of opposition from almost everybody else, they attacked the foundations of the entire post–Second World War international order. Such an action can have far-reaching consequences.

On March 15, 2003, on the eve of the US attack on Iraq, Professor Gwyn Prins of the London School of Economics wrote in *The Guardian*: "We are at the passing of the age of Middle Earth. All the agents and the institutions of that age will be profoundly affected. The previous breakpoint of equivalent importance was in the late 1940s. Emerging from the ashes of the destruction of the Third Reich, and led by the US, the victors found collective will to act, and in that time, they engendered the universal declaration of human rights and initiated the three main multilateral adventures of the next half-century: the UN, NATO, and the EU. Today, simultaneously, we are seeing the draining of power from all three, and transformation of the residuum. The catalyst to this profound and rapid change has been Iraq." He may well be right – and in that case, we are all in trouble.

The great achievement of the twentieth century was to make aggressive war illegal. People tend to sneer when they hear that assertion, since the twentieth century was obviously full of wars, but that's because they don't understand how very much worse the world was before we changed the rules. Few people realize that until the mid-twentieth century, it was perfectly legal for one country to attack, carve up, or even swallow another. Indeed, it was done all the time: at least 90 per cent of all the states that ever existed have been destroyed by war.

There have been interludes in various parts of the world where the impact of war was limited by common agreement. During the seventeenth and eighteenth centuries, for example, Europe fought its wars by a set of unwritten rules that prevented any of the great powers from going under (though countries as large as Poland could simply disappear, at least for a time). However, those rules broke down during the French Revolutionary and Napoleonic Wars of 1793–1815, when many smaller countries were simply swept away and even the biggest ones faced military occupation and regime change. Within the space of two years in 1812–14, there were French troops in Moscow and Russian troops in Paris. The badly shaken survivors of the Napoleonic Wars did manage to revive the old rules for the remainder of the nineteenth century – only to see them collapse entirely in the course of the First World War.

The 1914–18 war was not very different from the War of the Spanish Succession two hundred years earlier (1702–14) in its motives, its list of participants, or the stakes that the participants thought they were playing for when they entered the war: a colony here, a border province there, and of course prestige. But the mass death inflicted on conscript armies of ordinary citizens by the new weapons of industrialized slaughter during the Great War, as they called it at the time, was so great that the war had to be redefined as a cosmic struggle between good and evil. It gradually came to be seen that way in the minds of the warring populations and even of their leaders, not because the political stakes were unusually high or some great moral issue was involved, but because it was consuming hundreds of thousands of lives a month.

You can only justify the sacrifice of so many people by elevating your mundane war aims to an altogether higher level and transforming the struggle into a crusade against evil – but since it is impossible to compromise with evil, any possibility of a negotiated peace on the old pattern becomes impossible and diplomacy fails by definition. In the end, every regime on the losing side was destroyed, and two great empires of half a millennium's standing, Austria-Hungary and the Ottoman Empire, were chopped up into a dozen successor states.

"A general association of nations must be formed under specific convenants for the purpose of affording mutual guarantees of political independence and territorial integrity to great and small states alike."

– Woodrow Wilson, "Fourteen Points"
Speech to Congress, January 8, 1918

Whole populations were in shock by 1918. Matters had got so far out of hand that there was wide support for US president Woodrow Wilson's radical proposal that there should be new rules for international conduct and a new institution to enforce them: the League of Nations. It was duly created (though the US Congress refused to let the United States join) with the task of preventing further wars, especially among the great powers.

The League of Nations incorporated revolutionary ideas like the right of peoples to self-determination, and from the start it aroused a great deal of sullen resentment among the foreign policy professionals, who felt (as do today's American neo-conservatives) that the new institution in Geneva imposed unnecessary constraints on their freedom of action. Lord Robert Cecil, a strong supporter of the League, observed that the British government regarded it as "a kind of excrescence which must be carefully prevented from having too much influence on our foreign policy. Geneva, to them, was a strange place in which a newfangled machine existed to enable foreigners to influence or even to control our international action."

The League of Nations failed, of course, and not only because of the resistance of those who were still enmeshed in the old notions of absolute national sovereignty. It was born into a world where communist and fascist totalitarians vied for power in Europe, two-thirds of the planet's people lived in somebody else's empire, and the United States had retreated into isolationism. The idea of a forum where all the world's governments would be present all the time to deal with the world's problems collectively was a great leap forward, and preventing the outbreak of another war like the last was hugely important, but the League was doomed to fail.

The Italian invasion of Abyssinia (Ethiopia) in 1935, in defiance of the new international rules, showed that the great powers, despite their commitments, were in practice not ready to unite to prevent aggression. Multilateralism was a new and uncomfortable idea, and every country began to seek safety instead in private deals and alliances that quite closely mirrored those of the time before the First World War. Abandoning hope of multilateral action, Britain and France gave bilateral guarantees to Poland after Hitler seized the Czech lands in 1938; when he ignored those guarantees and invaded Poland in September 1939, it triggered the Second World War.

It is worth pausing at this point to consider what the League of Nations could have done about Hitler even if the United States had been a member and all the democracies had been willing to stand by its principles, for there is a great deal of naivete about the nature of both the League and its successor, the United Nations. If Adolf Hitler had confined himself to murdering Jews, gypsies, homosexuals, and domestic political opponents, and never invaded Poland or his other neighbours, he would have died in bed some time in the 1960s, and the Third Reich would have lasted until such time as the Germans themselves got sick of it.

The League's job was to prevent international aggression, not to police the behaviour of governments within their own borders, and it would have been against international law for the League to sponsor a military intervention to close down Dachau – not that it would have found any volunteers for the job. The democratic governments of Britain, France, and the United States would have wrung their hands and begged the Nazis to be nicer, but they would not have gone to war with Hitler over the concentration camps. They would probably even have gone on trading with Germany, so long as its leaders were reasonably discreet about the details of their extermination programme. Hitler's mistake was to attack and annex his neighbours and challenge the international balance of power.

If you doubt this, consider the fate of Stalin, who killed many millions more than Hitler but knew the international rules and was punctilious about observing them. Soviet troops occupied most of Eastern Europe at the end of the Second World War, but only with the consent of Moscow's allies, the other victorious great powers. The Soviet army forgot to go home again after that, but it never tried to move any farther west, so Stalin died a natural death, and his regime survived him by more than thirty years. It did so because the Soviet Union's rulers understood the basic rule of international law in an era of absolute sovereignty. You can do what you like to your own subjects, so long as you don't attack the neighbours. *Cuius regio, eius religio* (If he's your king, then that's your religion), as the Religious Peace of Augsburg put it in 1555, at the start of Europe's long domination over the world, and that is the way it has worked ever since.

So it would be a mistake to expect international law to protect you from your own government: the great twentieth-century experiment has been to see if it might at least be expanded to the point where it protects people from being killed by foreign governments. At the end of the Second World War, with some fifty-five million dead and half the cities of the developed world bombed flat, rebuilding an international organization that would be capable of taking on that job was the highest priority, and it was once again Americans who took the lead. The League was dead beyond hope of resurrection, but the surviving governments in 1945 went right out and cloned it (with some major improvements) as the United Nations Organization. They did it because they felt that they had to. One more great-power war like the one just past, but this time with every great power in possession of nuclear weapons from the start, and there would be nothing left. Changing the traditional way that the international system worked would be hard; not changing it would be fatal.

"More than an end to war, we want an end to the beginning of all wars – yes, an end to this brutal, inhuman and thoroughly impractical method of settling the differences between governments."

– President Franklin D. Roosevelt, April 1945

The United Nations as constituted in 1945 was a profoundly cynical organization, more explicitly so even than the League of Nations. It accepted without demur that its member states enjoyed absolute sovereignty and would never be forced to submit to intervention in their internal affairs (with the sole and uncertain exception that acts of genocide might trigger international intervention). The UN Charter made absolutely no moral or practical distinction between the most law-abiding democracies and the most repressive dictatorships among its membership. How could it, when more than half its members were themselves dictatorships? The UN was not about love, or justice, or freedom, although words of that sort are sprinkled freely through the preamble to the UN Charter; it was about avoiding another world war.

The problem that the surviving governments faced in 1945, in an even starker version than their predecessors in 1918, was this: the existing international system, which gives each sovereign state the right to use war as an instrument of policy, is bankrupt in an era of weapons of mass destruction. The world cannot afford to allow countries armed with nuclear weapons to go to war with each other.

It can certainly never again go through one of those generalized great-power mêlées (latterly called "world wars") that in the past were the main way of adjusting the international system to accommodate the changing balance between the great powers. If we fight that kind of war just once more, with thousands of nuclear weapons available to the major powers, the whole northern hemisphere will fry, so we have to stop doing it. We have to change the system. In fact, we have to outlaw war.

Because "outlaw war" sounds like a naive slogan on a protester's banner, people fail to grasp how radical a change it was for the great powers of the world to sign up to such a rule in 1945. Ever since the first city-states of Mesopotamia five thousand years ago, war had been a legitimate tool of statecraft, with no lasting opprobrium attached even to waging "aggressive war" so long as you were successful. Empires rose and fell, the militarily competent prospered, and the losers didn't get to write the history. Now, all of a sudden, it's over.

Since 1945, according to the UN Charter, it has been illegal to wage war against another country except in two tightly defined circumstances. One is that you have just been attacked, and are fighting back in immediate self-defence pending the arrival of international help. (There is no possible reading of this rule, Article 51 of the UN Charter, that would extend it to cover preventive war, where one country attacks another because of something it fears the other might do in future.) The other exception arises when the UN Security Council authorizes various member states to use military force on its behalf to roll back an aggression, or to enforce its decisions on a tightly limited number of other questions.

And that's it. Apart from these exceptions, international war – that is, war waged by a sovereign government across an international border – has been illegal since 1945. It is illegal to attack a country because it is sitting on territory that belonged to your country in your grandparents' time. It is even illegal to attack a country because it is ruled by a wicked dictator who oppresses his own people. The rules had to be written like that because to allow exceptions on these counts would have left loopholes big enough to drive a tank through – and because many of the countries that had to be persuaded to sign up in order for the new United Nations to become a truly universal organization were themselves ruled by wicked dictators who oppressed their own people. The founders of the UN in 1945 were not trying to create an organization that would impose democracy, justice, and brotherly love on the world. They were just trying to build an institution that would prevent a Third World War, and as many other wars as possible.

Making war illegal does not mean that all wars have stopped, any more than making murder illegal has stopped all killings, but it has transformed the context in which wars take place. The United Nations does not always act to roll back a successful aggression, because that requires getting past the vetoes wielded by all five per-manent members of the Security Council and then finding member states willing to put their troops at risk on the ground, but it almost never recognizes border changes that are accomplished by war.

For twenty-six years, it refused to recognize the annexation of East Timor by Indonesia as legal – and in the end, East Timor got its inde-pendence back. For twenty-four years, it refused to accept the occu-pation of South West Africa (now Namibia) by the apartheid regime in South Africa as legitimate, and in the end, Namibia got its inde-pendence too. For thirty-eight years it has refused to recognize the Israeli annexation of East Jerusalem after the 1967 war, even though nobody can currently imagine how that could ever be reversed. The point of the rule, quite explicitly, is that no country must ever profit territorially by its military success, for that would encourage further military adventures. And occasionally, as in Korea in 1950 or in Kuwait in 1990, the UN does manage to authorize an international military force to repel an aggression.

There is also, however, much that the UN cannot do. First and foremost, it cannot act against a perceived interest of any of the great powers, for in order to get them all to sign up it had to offer them a special deal: vetoes that allow the United States, Russia, Britain, France, and China to block any UN action they don't like. It's neither fair nor pretty, but how else were the founders of the UN going to get the great powers to sign up – and what use would the organization be if some of them were outside it?

In practice, the interlocking vetoes of the great powers on the Security Council meant that during the long years of the Cold War, when most world issues had been absorbed into the general confrontation between NATO and the Warsaw Pact, the UN was paralyzed in large parts of the world. It could only step in if both sides decided that getting the UN involved would enable them to back away safely from some dangerous confrontation (like the Cuban missile crisis) without loss of face.

The United Nations cannot intervene in a sovereign state – or at least it could not until recently – even to stop the most horrendous violations of human rights. The UN not only failed to intervene to stop the genocide in Cambodia in the late 1970s (for the Khmer Rouge, the perpetrators of that atrocity, were also the recognized sovereign government). It even continued to recognize the Khmer Rouge government-in-exile through most of the 1980s because it had been illegally displaced by a Vietnamese invasion. Matters might have been different if the United States, still bitter over its defeat by Vietnam, had not backed this policy so firmly, but in strict law the fact that the Vietnamese invasion had been intended in large part to stop the killing (particularly of the Vietnamese minority in Cambodia) simply did not count against the fact that Vietnam had violated the sovereignty of a neighbouring state.

And yet the UN is a central and indispensable part of the modern world. It is the institution through which a politically conscious global society first came into existence, and its specialized organs are still the arena in which most of the world's large-scale deals are made on matters ranging from telecommunications frequencies and trade to public health and the environment. It is the organizer and command centre for many of the peacekeeping missions that hold old enemies apart and try to minimize the level of violence in failed states, and the source of legal authority for most of those peacekeeping missions that it does not directly control. Since the end of the Cold War, it has become considerably more active in this field, in some cases even bending its own rules to ratify intervention in (smallish) sovereign states against the local government's will in order to end genocides and similar massive abuses of human rights. And most important by far, it is the repository of the new international law that bans the use of aggressive military force, even by the great powers.

It is not generally realized how important this law is because it is so often broken, especially by the really big powers. Repeatedly during the Cold War the superpowers of the time sponsored coups against the governments of recalcitrant countries within their own spheres of influence or even invaded them – the Soviet Union in Hungary, Czechoslovakia, and Afghanistan, the United States in Chile, Grenada, and Panama – and the lesser powers were not far behind. The British, French, and Israelis plotted to attack Egypt in the Suez War of 1956, Egypt and Syria launched a surprise attack on Israel in 1973, China fought border wars with both India and the Soviet Union, and India and Pakistan fought three wars of their own. Yet the fact that we now lived in a world where most of these actions were illegal did impose limitations on the traditional behaviour of states.

The superpowers disciplined their satellites without hindrance, but even they were careful to give lip service to international law in most cases: the Russians always found some local communist who could claim to be in power to invite them in when they invaded their satellites, and the United States went to the trouble of manufacturing a fake North Vietnamese naval attack on US ships in the Gulf of Tonkin before starting the bombing of North Vietnam. And most of the wars not backed by the veto-wielding superpowers lasted only a short time before international diplomatic intervention stopped them.

The Security Council would busy itself with appeals for a cease-fire and offers of peacekeeping troops, and at least one side (generally the one that was losing) would be eager to comply, which made it hard for the other side to go on fighting. So wars rarely ended in decisive victories any more, and territory almost never changed hands in a legal and permanent way no matter who won or who lost. These very significant constraints may also explain why nuclear weapons, which were used in the Second World War just as soon as they were invented, have not been used in war again for the past sixty years.

Of course, these same constraints can feel very burdensome if you happen to be the greatest power in the world, with overwhelming superiority in both nuclear and conventional weapons. You might even wind up filled with frustration and fury because all these Lilliput nations are trying to use the rules of the United Nations to tie you down like Gulliver.

The best measure of any institution's real importance is how much its enemies hate it. Richard Perle, a.k.a. the Prince of Darkness, house intellectual of the neo-conservative group since the mid-1980s and chairman of the Defense Policy Board at the Pentagon until allegations of conflict of interest compelled his resignation in early 2003, hates the UN a lot. In late March 2003, just as the US invasion of Iraq got underway – an invasion Perle and his fellow neo-conservatives hoped would destroy the Security Council's moral authority and its ability to put a brake on American power for good – he wrote an article for *The Spectator* in which he did a little jig of joy on the UN's presumptive grave. It is worth quoting at some length, because it gives a sense of the rage that the UN inspires in these circles.

> *Saddam Hussein ... will go quickly, but not alone: in a parting irony, he will take the UN down with him. Well, not the whole UN. The "good works" part will survive, the low-risk peacekeeping bureaucracies will remain, the chatterbox on the Hudson will continue to bleat. What will die is the fantasy of the UN as the foundation of a new world order. As we sift the debris, it will be important to preserve, the better to understand, the intellectual wreckage of the liberal conceit of safety through international law administered by international institutions ...*
>
> *[For many liberals], the thumb on the scale of judgment about this war is the idea that only the UN security council can legitimize the use of force ... This is a dangerously wrong idea that leads inexorably to handing great moral and even existential politico-military decisions to the likes of Syria, Cameroon, Angola, Russia, China and France ...*
>
> *Facing Milosevic's multiple aggressions, the UN could not stop the Balkan wars or even protect its [sic] victims ... We will not defeat or even contain fanatical terror unless we can carry the war to the territories from which it is launched. This will sometimes require that we use force against states that harbour terrorists, as we did in destroying the Taliban regime in Afghanistan. The most dangerous of these states are those that also possess weapons of mass destruction. Iraq is one, but there are others ... The chronic failure of the security council to enforce its own resolutions is unmistakable: it is simply not up to the task so we are*

left with coalitions of the willing. Far from disparaging them as a threat to a new world order, we should recognise that they are, by default, the best hope for that order, and the true alternative to the anarchy of the abject failure of the UN.

An invigorating rant by a master of sophistry, wonderfully compendious in its conflation of every half-truth, elision, and blatant lie that is deployed from time to time in arguments of this nature. There is the parochial sneer at the ridiculous idea of Americans having to share decisions on the fate of the world with countries "the likes of Syria, Cameroon, Angola, Russia, China and France." (But hang on a minute. If the United States is not willing to share those decisions with other great powers like Russia, China, and France, then it will have to compel their obedience by overwhelming military and financial power for the rest of eternity, and maybe have to fight them anyway in the end.)

There is the assertion that fighting fanatical terror "will sometimes require that we use force against states that harbour terrorists, as we did in destroying the Taliban regime in Afghanistan," as though this explains why the UN has become an obstacle to sane policy. Perle is counting on his readers to forget that the Security Council did effectively support military action against Afghanistan, agreeing that the United States had a legitimate case – and that since the war was not illegal, almost all the allies and friends of America who later baulked at joining the invasion of Iraq offered troops for the Afghan operation. There is the usual attempt to force Iraq into the same frame of reference by completely unsubstantiated and false assertions that it harboured terrorists and had weapons of mass destruction.

And so it goes on, with the UN portrayed one moment as an irrelevant excrescence and the next moment as an arrogant and uncaring organization of great power. Perle shamelessly serves up the familiar half-truth that "the UN could not stop the Balkan wars," as though it were an entity capable of acting independently of its most powerful member states. If it really were, then he would be the first to lead a revolt against it, but at this point in his argument it is a useful rhetorical device to mask the fact that it was the veto-wielding great powers on the Security Council – just as much the United States and Britain as Russia and China – that blocked the decisive use of UN-backed force to halt the fighting in the Balkans in 1992–95.

The failings of the UN in the Balkan Wars of the 1990s were the failings of the countries that made it up, and above all of the great powers with permanent seats on the Security Council. Since the Security Council is a veto-driven body, it can only be as determined to act as its most weak-kneed permanent member, which is a large problem if you have ambitions to see the UN become the full-time policeman of a new world order, fighting evil wherever it appears.

The problem is exactly the same, however, if you propose to fight evil instead with Richard Perle's "coalitions of the willing" – in the case of Iraq, the United States, Britain, and whichever countries they could beg, bully, or bribe into coming along. Just as there are some jobs that the Security Council will take on and others that it cannot agree upon, so there are some evils that Washington wants to fight, and others that it either doesn't care enough about – the Burmese dictatorship, for example – or does not dare take on, like North Korea or Iran.

In any case, the United Nations was not created to fight evil wherever it appears. It was designed primarily to stop the kind of straightforward cross-border aggression that had triggered both the First and the Second World Wars, but must not be allowed to cause a Third – and indeed, unprovoked invasions of the classic kind have been remarkably rare since 1945, presumably because the new international rules embodied in the UN Charter really do have some deterrent value. Since the veto-wielding permanent members of the Security Council stand to lose everything themselves in another world war, they have often been able to act in a surprisingly co-ordinated and decisive manner at the UN when events elsewhere threatened to drag them into such a conflict.

The first real test of the new rules came in June 1950, when North Korea invaded South Korea. The Security Council passed the test with flying colours, promptly authorizing the dispatch of a UN military force under American command that fought a three-year war to repel the aggression. True, that resolution probably only passed because the Soviet Union, North Korea's ally, was boycotting the Security Council at the time over the issue of who represented Chinese membership and therefore was not present to cast its veto.

Stalin in his final years was not wholly sane, and post-Soviet research in Russia suggests that he encouraged North Korea to invade the South. But Stalin's successors in the Soviet Union were generally as aware of their duty to avoid another world war as their Western counterparts, and when real crises came along the Security Council functioned fairly well. It managed to obtain rapid cease-fires in the various Arab–Israeli and Indo–Pakistani wars that dotted the last half of the twentieth century. On the other hand, the veto meant that it could take no collective stand on aggressions that occurred entirely within the sphere of influence of one of the superpowers themselves, like the Soviet invasion of Czechoslovakia in 1968 and the US invasion of Grenada in 1983. And the Security Council completely dodged the Iraqi invasion of Iran in 1980, mainly because both Washington and Moscow solidly supported Saddam Hussein's attack on his neighbour.

Saddam's subsequent invasion of Kuwait in 1990 was different, and not only because it threatened American interests in the Gulf. Although all Iraqi governments since independence had maintained a territorial claim to Kuwait, there was no recent history of tit-for-tat interventions and provocations as there had been between Iraq and Iran: the invasion of Kuwait came utterly out of the blue. It was one of the most blatant cases of unprovoked international aggression since Korea in 1950, and Saddam's declaration that he was annexing Kuwait compounded the offence: for the first time ever, a member of the UN was being conquered and absorbed by another member.

The situation was almost identical to the Italian invasion of Abyssinia in 1935 that had demonstrated the inability of the League of Nations to respond to aggression and so initiated the slide into the Second World War, and leaders who understood that history were determined that the United Nations should not go the same way as its predecessor. As it happened, the historically minded people in power at the time included Soviet president Mikhail Gorbachev and US president George H.W. Bush, both of whom were strongly committed to using the Security Council more vigorously to ensure global order in a post–Cold War world. So there was virtually no hesitation: the Security Council voted full legal authority for an American-led army to drive Saddam out of his conquest, and Bush did everything possible to ensure that the Gulf War of 1991 would be a useful precedent for future UN military operations to contain aggression and enforce international law. The elder Bush was a man of immense international experience – former US ambassador to China, former head of the Central Intelligence Agency, global business connections – and he actually understood the way the world works. In particular, he was conscious of the limitations of US power, the importance of restraint in military operations, and the absolute primacy of international law.

"We have before us the opportunity to forge for ourselves and for future generations a new world order – a world where the rule of law, not the law of the

jungle, governs the conduct of nations. When we are successful – and we will be – we have a chance at this new world order, an order in which a credible United Nations can use its peacekeeping role to fulfill the promise and vision of the UN's founders."

– President George H.W. Bush, announcing the
start of hostilities in the first Gulf War, January 16, 1991

Bush Sr. actually meant it too: what he was going to do in Iraq was precisely what the UN Security Council had authorized him to do, and not a bit more. "Trying to eliminate Saddam, extending the ground war into an occupation of Iraq ... would have incurred incalculable human and political costs," George Bush Sr. wrote in his 1998 book, *A World Transformed* (co-authored with his former national security adviser Brent Scowcroft). ". . . We would have been forced to occupy Baghdad and, in effect, rule Iraq. The coalition would instantly have collapsed, the Arabs deserting it in anger and other allies pulling out as well. There was no viable 'exit strategy' we could see, violating another of our principles. Furthermore, we had been self-consciously trying to set a pattern for handling aggression in the post-Cold War world. Going in and occupying Iraq, thus uni-laterally exceeding the United Nations mandate, would have destroyed the precedent of international response to aggression that we hoped to establish."

George Bush Sr. did not want Saddam Hussein to go on ruling in Iraq. He even encouraged rebellions against Saddam in the Shia south and Kurdish north of Iraq, although he probably regretted that in the end because without direct American support the revolts simply got a lot of people killed for nothing. (Most of the bodies found in the mass graves in Iraq after the 2003 invasion were people killed in the unsuccessful revolt against Saddam in 1991.) But he was unwilling to order US forces to invade Iraq and overthrow Saddam Hussein even though the road to Baghdad was open, because that would be going beyond the law.

The elder Bush also had grave reservations on a purely military level about going to Baghdad – "Had we gone the invasion route," he wrote in 1998, "the United States could conceivably still be an occupying power in a bitterly hostile land" – but his first concerns were the United Nations and international law. He believed that the end of the Cold War had created an opportunity for the UN Security Council to begin functioning as a real enforcer of international peace and order, and he was not going to throw that away by exceeding his legal mandate from the Security Council. When he spoke of a "New World Order," he really meant it. He had lived his whole adult life under the threat of a major nuclear war, and for him the strengthening of international law was an absolute priority. There was much more at stake than the fate of one tinpot dictator or even the fate of the Shia rebels, so once he reached the limit of his UN mandate to liberate Kuwait, he stopped.

Twelve years after George H.W. Bush fought a war to defend the sovereignty of Kuwait, his son George W. violated the sovereignty of Iraq and invaded and occupied the whole country without plausible provocation, legal justification, or Security Council approval. His administration had formally adopted a US national strategy of maintaining absolute military superiority over any rival power or combination of powers on the planet in perpetuity – an absurd ambition, but no less serious for all that. His challenge to the United Nations on the eve of his invasion of Iraq contained a scarcely hidden threat that the organization would henceforward be ignored by its most powerful member if it didn't follow Washington's lead: "All the world faces a test and the UN a difficult and defining moment. Will it serve the purpose of its founding [by giving Washington permission to attack Iraq], or will it be irrelevant?" And there was no coherent criticism of this blatant rejection of international law by the Democratic presidential candidate during the 2004 campaign either; just promises to pursue the same course more efficiently and with more attention to bringing important allies along. How did we get from the elder George Bush's "New World Order" to this desperate situation so fast?

It was not a straight downward path. In the afterglow of the successful Gulf War in 1991 and with better co-operation among the veto-wielding permanent members of the Security Council, there were several attempts to expand the UN's ability to intervene in armed conflicts beyond the limits laid down by the Charter. The various UN peacekeeping forces that had been sent to troubled corners of the world during the long decades of the Cold War had always gone at the request or at least with the consent of the "host" governments, since the UN's own rules forbade it to intervene in the affairs of sovereign member states without permission, but in the 1990s some peacekeeping missions and more robust "peace-enforcement" operations began to edge beyond the traditional boundaries.

The first of these, the ill-starred Somali intervention in 1992, was undertaken without any invitation or request for help from the host government because there simply wasn't any central government any more: Somalia had become a mere battlefield where rival militias fought amid a starving populace. In the minds of some of the authors of the action, in particular that of President George H.W. Bush, part of the attraction of "doing" Somalia may have been precisely that it gave the UN an opportunity to redefine and expand the nature of peacekeeping operations in a case that was not strictly illegal under the Charter. Nevertheless, it was an operation quite startling in its altruism, for none of the intervening powers had anything to gain from the intervention, nor did the chaos and misery of Somalia threaten any of their vital interests.

Unfortunately, it was also a very difficult operation in an

intensely hostile environment. For the United States, which lost eighteen soldiers killed in a single day in Mogadishu in an ill-advised and badly managed raid (the "Black Hawk down" episode) that also killed up to a thousand Somalis, it ended up being perceived as an abject failure. One of President Bill Clinton's first acts in office in 1993 was to pull the whole US force out of Mogadishu, and the experience left such deep scars on the new administration that Clinton flatly refused to allow the UN to mount a major military operation in Rwanda in 1994 to stop the genocide there. It was not so easy to ignore the savage wars that began to wreck the countries of former Yugoslavia in the early 1990s, however, and gradually and reluctantly Clinton's administration was drawn back into the business of military intervention.

The Balkan military interventions of the 1990s – Bosnia in 1995 and Kosovo in 1999 – were undertaken in a quite different political atmosphere from Somalia. They were in a part of the world where the great powers had major political and security interests (and even, in the case of the Russians, strong emotional ties). They ran straight up against the ban on UN intervention in the internal affairs of sovereign states: Serbian dictator Slobodan Milosevic was a vicious sponsor of ethnic cleansing and mass murder, but he was definitely the legitimate ruler of a sovereign state, and bombing Serbia to make him stop what he was doing definitely constituted intervention in its internal affairs. Russia, where public opinion is instinctively pro-Serb and anti-Muslim for historical reasons, and China, which is perennially nervous about any change in the rules about sovereignty that might expose it to future intervention, were both reluctant to authorize offensive military operations in the Balkans under UN auspices, and at first the United States and Britain were equally opposed.

Nothing could legally be done to stop the slaughter of Muslims by forces operating with Milosevic's tacit approval in Bosnia and later in Kosovo – yet something had to be done. The solution, once the Clinton administration got over Somalia and worked its nerve up for another intervention, was to wage limited air-only wars against Serbia using "coalitions of the willing" (in practice, the forces of the NATO alliance) that operated on a nod-and-a-wink basis, with the unspoken understanding that these operations would receive UN approval after the fact. The Kosovo War in 1999 was a particularly dodgy business from the legal point of view because Kosovo, unlike Bosnia, was still part of Serbia and so the horrors there were, strictly speaking, a Serbian domestic affair.

NATO undertook the Kosovo operation only because all the major powers understood that the Russian government, while obliged by public opinion at home to veto any proposal for military action against Serbia that came before the Security Council, wasn't really planning to die in a ditch to stop it from happening. It was virtually certain that the Russian government, which was run by quite sensible people, would allow the UN to take ownership of the occupation and retrospectively legitimize the war once the shooting stopped – and so would the Chinese government, which had no wish to isolate itself further in a world where every other major power is at least formally democratic.

If it was acceptable for NATO to attack Serbia over Kosovo in 1999 without Security Council authority, on the assumption that the legal details could be tidied up later, then why was it wrong for the United States to invade Iraq without UN authority in 2003? The answer is that in 2003 there was not even tacit support for the US action among a majority of the members of the Security Council.

When the UN's members, driven mainly by humanitarian considerations, began to stretch the rules against outside intervention in the internal affairs of sovereign states after the end of the Cold War, they did so on the understanding that it would always be done on the basis of a broad consensus, and there was no such consensus on

Iraq. On the contrary, few governments believed the Bush administration's allegation that Iraq represented a threat to world peace urgent enough to justify the unprovoked invasion of an independent country, nor was the humanitarian situation there any worse than it had been for the previous ten or twenty years. Other countries simply did not believe Washington's "evidence" or trust its motives, so the Bush administration went to war virtually alone.

In attacking Iraq in March 2003, Washington not only violated international law, but it also abandoned the multilateral consensus that had more or less legitimized the various attempts to move beyond the strict UN rules in the name of humanitarian intervention during the 1990s. There are those who would argue, with the wisdom of hindsight, that those attempts to move beyond the old ban on invading a sovereign state even for humanitarian reasons were therefore a mistake, since they gave Washington a precedent of sorts to work with. However, this argument implicitly assumes that the Bush administration actually cared about the UN rules and merely wanted to expand the scope for legal intervention further to embrace cases like Iraq. This was not the case.

"I think in this case international law stood in the way of doing the right thing ... [There was] no practical mechanism consistent with the rules of the UN for dealing with Saddam Hussein ... International law ... would have required us to leave Saddam Hussein alone."

– Richard Perle, November 20, 2003

The real ambition of the neo-conservatives who came to power with George W. Bush, frankly expressed in their speeches and writings, was to sweep aside all impediments to the unilateral exercise of American power, starting with the legal authority of the Security Council. Many of them were therefore quietly pleased when the United States ended up invading Iraq illegally and virtually alone apart from Britain: that helped to drive home to everybody the fact that America's actions were showing the United Nations to be, in Bush's favourite word, "irrelevant." In a nod to the old rules, the US government's international lawyers did throw up a legal smoke-screen of claims that the United States was free to attack Iraq without explicit UN authorization on the basis of old Security Council resolutions dating back to before the first Gulf War in 1991, but there was scarcely an independent expert on international law in the world who accepted those claims – and the neo-conservatives couldn't have cared less.

So they got their war, and of course they won it easily (annual US military spending was about 140 times greater than Iraq's). To a considerable extent, they also succeeded in sidelining the United Nations, which lacked the ability to stop the American action and realized that it would be counter-productive to condemn it openly. But if the UN sinks into irrelevance, what replaces it? Will the other countries of the world – the other 96 per cent of the human race – accept the unilateral exercise of US power as an adequate substitute for the rule of law in international affairs? Certainly not.

The entire international community is now in a state of suspended animation. Most other governments deplore what the Bush administration did, but they are so appalled by the choices they would have to make if this turns out to be a permanent new reality that they have effectively put their foreign policy on hold. They continue to believe that the United Nations is our only real bulwark against a return to the lethal old world of international anarchy, and they do not want to abandon the work of sixty years in response to the actions of a unilateralist US policy that might prove to be only a passing phase in America's adjustment to the changing global balance of power. They even devised a strategy of sorts for trying to shepherd the United States back inside the system without a confrontation.

In October 2003, the Security Council passed a unanimous resolution that recognized US responsibility to hand over control to a new Iraqi government as soon as possible, and in June 2004 it passed a further resolution recognizing the "sovereign government" that the United States had selected to replace direct US rule. On the surface, it looked as if the invasion of Iraq had been just another Kosovo-style exercise where a "coalition of the willing" was given a nod and a wink from the UN to do the job, with legitimation after the fact by the Security Council a foregone conclusion. But it was nothing of the sort.

The United States was given the quasi-legitimation of the two post-war Security Council resolutions on Iraq because the only real alternative would have been to condemn the organization's most powerful member as an international outlaw. Such an action would have elicited only defiance and abuse from the Bush administration, and would have alienated precisely the American voters on whom everybody else was counting to remove the Bush administration in November 2004. Better to paper over cracks for the moment and pretend that the United States was still committed to the United Nations – though it will be noted that the two resolutions shook loose very little new money and virtually no extra non-American troops for the US occupation forces in Iraq.

But time is running out on these stalling tactics. If the neo-conservatives and radical nationalists in the administration retain their stranglehold on American defence and foreign policy, then within a few years other major countries will probably start moving to protect their own interests by creating countervailing centres of power. They will not be called alliances at first, but that is what they may become.

"A war which lacks legitimacy does not acquire legitimacy if it is won ... We have a vision of the world based on the view that war should not be used to

settle a crisis which can be resolved by other means. War must be the ultimate resort. The world today obliges us to seek a consensus when we act, and not to act alone.

"The US has a vision of the world which is very unilateralist. I hold a vision of a multilateral world which apparently – and I say apparently – is opposed to this. Europe is, and certainly will be in the future, here to stay as a major world power. Then we have to take account of the emergence of China on the world stage, and India too ... Whether you like it or not, whether you want it or not ... we are moving towards a multipolar world."

– French president Jacques Chirac, at the
G8 Summit, Evian, France, May 25, 2003

You can live safely in a multipolar world that has multilateral reflexes and a respect for international law, but great-power politics is lethally dangerous in a multipolar world with no effective international institutions. The Cold War was a bipolar world with a partially effective UN as a buffer between the two blocs, and the 1990s was a time of unprecedented international amity when it could truly be said that no great power had good reason to fear the intentions of any other. The best recent historical parallel for the process we may soon embark upon is the early twentieth century, when the alliances that later fought the First World War initially took shape.

There was a paramount power, Britain, that had allowed itself to become isolated. There were anxious established powers that had already been in relative decline for some time: France, Austria-Hungary, and Turkey. There were ambitious rising powers: Germany, Russia and Japan. There was absolutely no system of collective security – countries were free to attack one another, seize colonies, and even annex parts of each other's homelands – so the only way to protect yourself was to band together with other countries in alliances. And there was a very gradual, often secretive process in which the major powers did move into alliances over a period of years. Any resemblance between this history and the process that we may embark upon in the next ten years is all too plausible.

History does not repeat itself, but patterns of international behaviour do. In a world where the UN has been gutted and the law of the jungle has returned, you would expect nations to respond by increasing armaments and forming something like the alliances that emerged in the years before 1914. That does not mean that the public will read about it when it happens, or that these new arrangements will be formal alliances like NATO and the old Warsaw Pact, with joint military command centres and the like. Indeed, the husk of NATO may survive, like the Holy Roman Empire of former times, even as its members informally align themselves with new partners – and *informal* is probably the key word if we go through this pattern again, for formal military alliances with no ideological cement have been unfashionable for a long time. Even a hundred years ago, the arrangement between Russia, France, and Britain, though in reality an alliance, was known simply as the "Friendly Understanding" (Entente Cordiale).

It's not all that hard to guess what the global lineup would be *circa* 2015 if Washington continues to pursue its unilateral fantasy of absolute power and there is a global retreat from multilateralism. The choice of potential alliance partners is never that wide for any country, as it is driven by geography, shared concerns about the behaviour of certain other countries, and the question of whether a given relationship is a good military and political fit.

Every single alliance relationship that is sketched out below has been a reality at some point in the past 150 years, with the sole exception of the United States and India.

NATO would certainly be the first victim of a realignment of the great powers, though it is not true that "the Atlantic is getting wider," as some claim: the body of water that is rapidly expanding is the English Channel. Of NATO's three militarily significant

European members, France and Germany have taken the lead in opposing the trend of American policy since 2001, while Britain remains indissolubly wedded to the United States not only by the Blair government's choice but more profoundly through its dependence on the United States for key elements in its "independent" nuclear deterrent force. Although many people in Britain feel very uncomfortable about it, the Anglo-American alliance, now almost a century old, will probably remain as firm in any plausible future that starts from here as it was in Orwell's *Nineteen Eighty-Four* (where Britain was Oceania's "Airstrip One" off the coast of Eurasia).

America's other allies in this changed world would include Canada (whether it likes it or not), Australia, Israel (by far the greatest military power in its own region despite its small population) – and perhaps India. This is a world in which the American military presence in the Muslim Middle East would persist and might even expand, with possible invasions of Syria and Iran following those of Afghanistan and Iraq to create a solid block of US–controlled territory from the eastern border of Israel to the western border of Pakistan. Since India's immediate security concerns focus mainly on Pakistan and to a lesser extent on other Muslim countries that back Pakistan in the Kashmir dispute, it would be hard for any Indian government to resist the temptation to throw its lot in with an America that had effectively subjugated its Muslim near-neighbours. It would be equally hard for the United States to resist the attraction of Indian military manpower if it were bogged down in a series of occupations of Middle Eastern countries (though this raises the question of what would become of America's current alliance with nuclear-armed Pakistan). An Indo-American alliance is a particularly good fit because strategists of a traditional bent in both countries see China as their emerging strategic rival, in India's case for dominance in Asia and in the US case for global dominance.

President Bush's National Security Strategy statement of 2002, seeking to provide a rationale for "containing" China, argued that Beijing was leading the dance and Washington was merely reacting: "In pursuing advanced military capabilities that can threaten its neighbours in the Asia-Pacific region, China is pursuing an outdated path." (As if the United States had ceased to pursue advanced military capabilities.) But the reality is that US policy in this area, as in so much else, has been preemptive, actively seeking an alliance with India against China.

The Bush administration began courting India as soon as it took office, appointing one of the "Vulcans," Robert Blackwill, as US ambassador to New Delhi. The post-9/11 panic gave the White House an excuse to end the sanctions that had been imposed on India and Pakistan after their 1998 nuclear weapons tests, and by 2003 India and the United States were conducting joint military exercises. The ten-year Indo-US military agreement signed in June, 2005, did not create a formal military alliance, but it came very close, with provisions for large-scale Indian arms purchases and co-production agreements, promises of Indian access to next-generation American weapons, and arrangements for joint exercises and naval patrols, American training for Indian carrier pilots, and close consultation on security matters.

Viewed from Beijing, the Indo-US agreement looks very much like the final step in an American plan to encircle China with hostile alliances. Beijing's response so far has been quite moderate, in part because there are no obvious counter-alliances it can make – no other major power would feel comfortable in forging a close political relationship with the bizarre post-Communist autocrats who currently rule China – and partly because other major powers are working quite hard to keep China from feeling isolated and cornered. That's the main reason why France, in early 2004, became the first European country to conduct joint naval exercises with China, and why European Union chief Romano Prodi made sure that China has access to data from Europe's planned satellite geo-positioning system (which would enable Beijing to target its missiles more accurately). In the same spirit, Russia conducted its first joint military exercises with China in August, 2005. But these gestures are not precursors to some European–Chinese strategic alliance. Quite apart from the political gulf between democratic Europe and autocratic China, the sheer scale of China makes the whole business of building an alliance less urgent in Beijing's eyes, and its rapid growth towards full industrialized country status reinforces its go-it-alone distaste for alliance games.

Beijing has been playing a very long game since the death of Deng Xiao-ping, seeking to avoid any confrontation with the established great powers and especially with the United States while it grows back into great-power status itself. But at a certain point the aggressive promotion of *Pax Americana* would invalidate this strategic policy: China would definitely act to constrain the unilateral exercise of American power in its part of the world, where unresolved questions about the future of Taiwan and North Korea offer plenty of potential for confrontation. If there's a return to the old world with the old rules, then China would urgently build up its own military power, including most especially its nuclear deterrent power. It was genuine restraint, not lack of resources, that held China back all these years: it built no more than a couple of hundred nuclear-tipped missiles, of which as few as eighteen had the range to strike at the United States, because it genuinely believed that even such a small force was enough to deter anybody contemplating a nuclear strike against China in the relatively benign strategic circumstances of the time. If nobody was actually planning to attack China, why waste more money on deterrence? But China was never so poor that it could not afford to build thousands of long-range nuclear missiles, and there is no law or treaty that would prevent it from doing so if it felt the need.

This would leave us with not a two- but a three-bloc world, for it is hard to imagine that either the Western Europeans or the Russians would find an alliance with China attractive or even comfortable. However, they might well make an alliance with each other. Within the European Union, France and Germany were already moving towards closer military and political co-ordination outside the NATO framework, but even with the addition of most of the smaller members of the European Union, a Franco-German alliance would not counter-balance the military and economic power of the United States. Paris and Berlin would have to find a great-power partner with a big resource base and a serious nuclear weapons capability, and the obvious candidate is Russia.

Would Russia be attracted by such an alliance? Moscow greatly prefers the current world where it is not forced to choose between the United States and Europe, but in the end the Russian leadership knows that it is European. Its great unspoken ambition for the past dozen years has been to join the European Union, and the reward that the Western European great powers could offer in exchange for EU access to Russia's huge natural resources and nuclear weapons capabilities is accelerated EU membership (though it might by then be membership in a European Union that has lost the United Kingdom). If Russia concludes that its dream of a real partnership with Washington, even a junior partnership, is just a fantasy – and it is already pretty close to that conclusion – then a Paris–Berlin–Moscow deal is not a far-fetched alternative.

There have already been cautious diplomatic explorations of this strategic option. In the months after the invasion of Iraq, Paris and Berlin began for the first time to talk seriously of a "union of France and Germany" that would merge their foreign and defence policies. (Dominique de Villepin, then France's foreign minister and now its prime minister, called it "the only historic gamble that we cannot possibly lose.") If it came into existence, such an entity, with about 140 million people, would be able to approach Russia (population 145 million) as an equal in any discussions about a possible alliance – and such discussions, in the most tentative and informal way, may already have taken place. In July 2003, Alain Juppé, a former French prime minister and foreign minister who was then the leader of President Chirac's reformed Gaullist party, visited Moscow. What was said in private is not known, but Juppé afterwards commented that "the idea of a strategic partnership between the European pole and the Russian pole" did not exclude "dialogue with the other poles, the American pole, of course, and China." And he added: "The world of the coming decades will function this way."

This would give pleasure to some in France, where it is commonplace to discuss NATO as "a tool to prevent Europe from having a common defence," but it would not please most Germans or Russians. The German election of October, 2005, which led to a "grand coalition" government incorporating both major parties, made any early movement even on a Franco-German union much less likely, and Juppé's notion of a "strategic partnership between the European pole and the Russian pole" has now been placed on a distant back burner while the prospective strategic partners wait to see which way the United States jumps. But they could make such an alliance work if they felt they had to, and it could grow into a serious strategic competitor to the United States in less than a decade.

As for the "New Europe" (as Donald Rumsfeld called it) of former Soviet-bloc countries in Eastern Europe whose governments have aligned themselves with the United States over Iraq, they would have little choice but to go along with this sort of continental European alliance in the end. They want to be in the EU even more than they mistrust the Russians, and a large majority of their own citizens already strongly opposes the commitments their governments have made to support American policy in the Middle East.

Among the major players there remains only Japan, whose relatively isolated and invulnerable position suggests that its future may be that of a giant Asian Switzerland, heavily armed but increasingly neutral. Other middle powers like Italy, Spain, Turkey, and South Korea, currently in US–led alliances, would have a difficult time deciding where their future lies, though the first three would probably end by opting for Eurasia. This would be an inherently unstable situation, since it would mean that much or most of the Middle East was effectively US–occupied territory, but for quite a long while, nothing terrible might happen.

In sketching out this possible world of ten years hence, I am drawing a not-quite-worst-case scenario that may never come to pass. It is possible that a change of course or of administration in Washington will quickly return us to the relatively safe and orderly world of the later 1990s, with little to remind us of this interlude except the mess in Iraq and a heightened consciousness about the risk of terrorist attacks. But if these informal alliances do begin to take shape, then the level of trust in the world will go down dramatically – think how short a time it took during the runup to the invasion of Iraq for many Americans to become persuaded that France, of all places, was their enemy – and vicious circles of entirely familiar historical types will start to rotate. At that point we would be in a situation that is probably more dangerous, though less overtly hostile, than the Cold War.

It would be less overtly hostile because the immense movements of people, goods, and money around the world that are the hallmark of this globalized era would not cease, though they might diminish, and because international information flows would continue to be relatively free, if only for economic reasons. It would be a situation reminiscent of the early twentieth century, another globalized, free-trading era when most ordinary people did not even need passports to move between countries – but the level of international mistrust was very high, and the lethal military calculations of the alliances lurked behind the peaceful facade of everyday life. The danger is not that some madman might launch a deliberate war of conquest; it is that various governments would begin to worry once again that local clashes between the alliances or their proxies might escalate, and that threats might be made which must be deterred to preserve their credibility, and that they therefore have to think about what they would do in the face of the awful contingency that deterrence doesn't work or that somebody misunderstands. . .

Neither of the great alliances of the Cold War ever seriously considered launching an all-out nuclear attack against the other except as "pre-emption" of an anticipated surprise attack, usually in the midst of some escalating local crisis, but they still came quite close to war a number of times. If only evil dictators bent on world conquest began wars, we would be fairly safe, but a belief that pre-emption ("first strike," as they called it back then) might mean survival for the people on our side can persuade even normally sane and moral people that destroying millions of foreigners' lives with nuclear weapons is a rational option. The psychologists who regularly tested the crews in the missile silos for reliability during the Cold War looked for exactly that sort of rationalization in their clients, and they had no trouble finding it. They probably still don't.

For more than half a century, far-sighted people in many countries have been working on a project for international law and order that is our best and perhaps our only chance of avoiding global disaster on an unprecedented scale. It is obviously a hundred-year project at the very least, for it flies in the face of history and of traditional ideas about human nature, as most of its supporters were well aware from the start. They had to try anyway, because all the alternative outcomes were so much worse in a world of nuclear weapons, and they have made encouraging progress towards their goal. By the late 1990s it was becoming possible to believe that the project might actually succeed, and that the worst of the horrors that infested our future might never come to pass. Now all that is at risk.

CHAPTER VI

SURVIVING THE
TWENTY-FIRST CENTURY

"This is a century which is going to see China emerge as the largest economy, and usually with economic power comes military clout. In the world we are constructing, we want to know [that the system] will work whoever is the biggest and the most powerful. It would be very easy for a country like New Zealand to make excuses and think of justifications for what its friends were doing, but we would have to be mindful that we were creating precedents for others also to exit from multilateral decision making. I don't want [those] precedents set, regardless of who is seen as the biggest kid on the block.

"We saw the UN as a fresh start for a world trying to work out its problems together rather than a return to a nineteenth-century world where the great powers carved it up ... Who wants to go back to the jungle?"

– Helen Clark, prime minister of New Zealand, May 2003

New Zealand refused to send its troops to join the United States, Britain, and Australia in invading Iraq because Helen Clark's government understood that what we do now affects the future. The day will come when the United States is no longer the superpower bestriding the world, but New Zealand's geography will always be the same as it is now, so it needs a global system that will protect it from harm even when China is the greatest power: a system based on law and multilateral consensus. So does everybody else.

It's not hard to run the world when things are as easy as they are now. There is an established set of great powers, their relative rankings virtually unchanged for the past fifty years except for the Russians, who have accepted their fall from superpower status with remarkable grace. There are no rival alliance systems, and no great power has a major grievance against any other. The global economic climate is benign, the physical climate is not yet changing radically, and painful decisions that require serious sacrifices can still be postponed. A world where terrorism is seen as the biggest problem is a world without big problems. But this happy scene is going to change.

Global warming and other environmental problems are going to hit us very hard over the next fifty years. How fast they will hit, and how great the resulting upheavals will be, cannot be known in advance, but very few people apart from the usual suspects in the

United States any longer doubt that climate change is a reality, and that it will hurt some countries a lot more than others. There will probably be major disruptions in food supply and mass movements of population in some parts of the world – including some technologically competent parts of the world that have access to the full range of modern weapons. It will not be possible to ignore their suffering, as they will possess the means of drawing it forcefully to everybody else's attention, so there had better be a system in place that enables us to spread the burden of coping with these changes.

At the same time, the pecking order of the great powers is starting to change again. In a globalized world where regional differences in the level of education, technological ability, and commercial competitiveness are gradually being erased, small countries with a big lead like Portugal in the sixteenth century or Britain in the nineteenth century can no longer be in the first rank of the great powers; only countries of a semi-continental scale can be contenders. The five biggest powers of 2040 will be China, the United States, India, Russia, and Brazil – probably in that order. This ranking is implicit in the current long-term growth rates of these economies, projected one generation out, and while some specific country might surprise us by growing faster or slower than the projections suggest, the overall pattern is practically carved in stone.

The last time the world went through a change of this order, it ended up in the First World War. Long before we get to 2040 – within the next ten years, in all likelihood – the strains and stresses that these gradual shifts in relative power are putting on the existing great-power system will begin to show through. If we have a working multilateral system in place, these stresses and strains can probably be contained and channelled, and everybody will have time to accommodate themselves to the emerging realities gradually and peacefully. If not, then we may look forward to a process quite similar to that before the First World War, with everybody seeking shelter in alliances of one sort or another.

It would be a less stable situation than the Cold War, for that was a relatively simple time where there were only two blocs, when the threat of nuclear weapons proliferation beyond the five declared nuclear powers had been largely contained, and when terrorists were a good deal less imaginative than they are now. Getting through the next half-century was going to be tricky enough even if the great powers went on trusting one another and the United Nations worked well. It will be hopeless if we end up in alliances and arms races again, but the current US bid to impose a new and unwelcome *Pax Americana* on the world could set off a slide back into that old pattern and foreclose on our future.

The risk is compounded by the very fragile state of the US economy. The US dollar's prolonged act of levitation is already faltering, and the possibility that it will end in a sudden crash cannot be excluded. Just as it is in everybody else's interest to offer the United States a non-humiliating path of retreat out of Iraq (hence the unanimous UN resolutions of October 2003 and June 2004), so it is in the interest of investors and central banks everywhere that the dollar does not suddenly collapse, and they will do what they can to avoid it. But if it happens anyway, there could be an extreme political reaction in the United States. It cannot be presumed that blame would automatically be cast on the right culprits. Indeed, it can safely be assumed that there would be an enormous political effort in the United States to shift the blame onto foreigners, accompanied by a steep increase in American popular hostility towards those countries that are seen as having opposed US policy internationally.

It could get quite ugly, in other words, and we could end up with a world we do not like a bit. The objective is to get through what prom-ises to be a very difficult half-century without a world war, and what happens in the next couple of years may be decisive. Either we get back to building the international institutions we started working on sixty years ago, or we get used to the idea that we are working our way up to the Third World War. So it is important that the United States does not succeed in turning Iraq into a Middle Eastern base for *Pax Americana*, and that Americans come to see the whole project for global hegemony as an expensive mistake. But it is also important that other countries give the United States the softest possible landing. Not only does the world not need an angry and resentful America, it needs a United States that is actively committed to the project for building a law-based international society.

"There were times when it appeared that American power was seen to be more dangerous than Saddam Hussein. I'll just put it very bluntly. We just didn't understand it."

– Condoleezza Rice, May 30, 2003

At the G8 Summit after the invasion of Iraq, Condoleezza Rice was like a schoolteacher reading out the end-of-term reports for a group of children who had failed to live up to their potential. "There was disappointment that a friend like Canada was not able to support the US on what we considered a very important issue," she said. "There was disappointment in the response of the German government, too." And the behaviour of France was "particularly disappointing." It was ridiculous, but it was also very revealing. The United States had just carried out an entirely unprovoked and illegal act of aggression, everybody else knew that it was bound to end in tears – and yet Rice felt fully justified in rebuking them for failing to go along with it. It suggested an almost total inability to see the administration she served and its policies as others saw them.

It was not an isolated incident. The neo-conservatives never intended the United States to become as isolated as it has. They imagined that when they displayed American "resolve" and demonstrated that they were now in sole charge of the planet through an exemplary war or two against universally unpopular regimes, all their old friends and allies would fall into line under *Pax Americana* more or less willingly. They were not supposed to respond as they have. Nobody in Washington in 2001 could have imagined that only two years later half of the European Union's citizens (according to an 18,000-person, 15-country survey conducted six months after the invasion of Iraq) would see the United States as a danger to world peace rather than a force for good.

This peculiar inability to predict the responses of others is largely due to the very enclosed world in which American debate on these issues has taken place in recent years. From Samuel Huntington's *The Coming Clash of Civilizations* in the mid-1990s – immensely influential in the Washington bureaucracy and various think-tanks that were desperately seeking a new enemy, but mostly seen as high-brow propaganda outside the United States – to Robert Kagan's 2003 book, *Paradise and Power*, which explains that the United States must take over the world but the Europeans won't understand why because "Americans are from Mars, Europeans are from Venus," the key books and articles that have set the intellectual tone inside the Beltway in Washington have addressed a world that bears little resemblance to reality as experienced by most non-Americans.

The fact is that neither Europeans nor Asians nor (above all) Middle Easterners agree with mainstream American political opinion any more. They don't think al-Qaeda is a global menace. They don't live in fear of rogue states. They don't think we are living in the opening stages of a "clash of civilizations" (though they worry that Washington's efforts might yet make it happen). They don't agree with pre-emptive and preventive wars, and they don't believe that 9/11 "changed everything." And no amount of lecturing by American officials and academics who tell them to "grow up" is going to change that. It is a genuine difference of perspective, not anti-

Americanism – but pushing *Pax Americana* much further could turn it into that.

Meanwhile, what about the poor Iraqis?

"I tell you, it is never boring in Baghdad these days … You go out of your house in the morning never knowing if you will get to work at all. Some days it is bad: huge checkpoints with tanks, where everybody has to get out of their cars. What is amazing is that the Americans have still not learned their lesson and always bring just one translator – actually, strike that: the translators have stopped going to work, so we are lucky if there is one at all …

"The weather is fine, and when the sun sets we sit in an outdoor tea-house listening to pro-Fallujah songs blasting from a car stereo while teenagers stand beside the car trying to look tough. If we get sick of that we go to a friend's newly opened mobile-phone accessory shop in Adhamiya, where he has to dodge demands for phone covers with pictures of Saddam on them. Even more surreally, a kid came in asking if he had any of the old 'Saddam, we love you' songs that he could use as a ring tone.

"Did I tell you that I don't understand my country any more?"

– "Salam Pax," *The Guardian*, May 5, 2004

Iraqis are not the passive, helpless people whose allotted role in the neo-conservative fantasy was first to stand cheering by the side of the road while the US army liberated them and then to receive "freedom" and democracy gratefully from American hands. (And, of course, to make fourteen permanent military bases in their country available to the US armed forces in partial recompense for this American generosity.) Iraq used to be the most literate of all the big Arab countries, and in the 1970s, before Saddam's wars impoverished the country, it was also the most developed and prosperous of the large Arab states, with a big middle class, a diversified economy, and social services of a near-European standard. It could be all of those things again, and democratic to boot – and it does not need American tutelage to get there.

Nobody needs American tutelage to get there. Democracy is not a copyrighted American process that can be implanted elsewhere by force. It is a way of running the affairs of large societies that is available to anybody who wants it, regardless of their particular culture, and the history of the past twenty years demonstrates that people of every culture want it and know how to get it: Filipinos, Bangladeshis, South Koreans, Russians, South Africans, Indonesians – and, one of these days, Arabs too. It could easily take root in Iraq, but it has to be left to the Iraqis. It cannot come as part of a package that also involves making Iraq an American client state, because that makes those who are in power collaborators and discredits any project with which they are associated.

The wave of violence that has swept over Iraq since the American occupation does include a number of attacks by Islamist terrorists who have been attracted to the country by the presence of American forces, but it is primarily a homegrown resistance movement driven by anger at the American presence. A more competent occupation regime than the chaotic Coalition Provisional Authority might have postponed the growth of a resistance movement – disbanding the Iraqi army and turning several hundred thousand military men out on the streets *with their weapons* has to rank among the ten stupidest decisions of the past century – but if it had not emerged now, then the United States would have pressed ahead even more determinedly with its plan to turn Iraq into its main Middle Eastern base, and the resistance would just have emerged a bit later, as America's plans for Iraq became clearer. One way or another, the American military presence was going to elicit an Iraqi resistance movement.

What would happen if the United States just pulled its troops out? Not necessarily the civil war that US propaganda insists is the only alternative to a continuing American military presence in Iraq. There have been bitter clashes between predominantly Arab governments in Baghdad and separatist-minded Kurds on a number of occasions in the past (and that could happen again whether the United States stays or goes), but Arab Iraq has never had a civil war. Politics was an extremely rough game in Iraq during the forty-five years between the overthrow of the British-imposed king in 1958 and the destruction of the Baathist regime by US military power in 2003, but Iraqis always understood that they were all in the same boat and that it made no sense to sink it. There was no civil war then, and it's not clear why there would be one now.

If American troops were to leave, it would certainly help if UN troops, preferably from Muslim countries, were arriving at the same time, because there is a genuine problem of public security in Iraq. But even if other countries refuse to send their soldiers into Iraq now that things have got so far out of hand, the American troops should still go – and go very fast. The Iraqis may not succeed in composing their differences peacefully and refounding their country as a democratic state, but their chances of doing so are far greater if they do not have to contend with the American occupation and the violent resistance to it. As for the "war on terror," Iraq was the wrong place to fight it anyway, but more generally it must be taken away from the armed forces and given back to the people who really should be waging it, the intelligence services and police forces of the world.

And if all this happens, what becomes of America's position in the world? No more dreams of global hegemony, obviously, but the United States remains the first among equals for at least another generation. None of the other great powers wants to take that role away from it; they just want it to play by the rules, and carry its share of the load in building an international system that is capable of withstanding the storms that are coming.

"It is ... a trait no other nation seems to possess in quite the same degree that

we do – namely, a feeling of almost childish injury and resentment unless the world as a whole recognizes how innocent we are of anything but the most harmless and generous intentions."

– Eleanor Roosevelt (wife of President Franklin D. Roosevelt), 1946

The hardest thing Americans are going to have to do in this generation is to get used to the idea that the United States is just another country. Still a very big and powerful country, to be sure, but not the "indispensable nation," not a beacon of liberty shining into the darkness, and not the only great power that really matters. Most other countries are now democratic too, and they do not look to the United States for example. No other country yet rivals the United States in military power, but that is not as important as Americans think because their enormous military machine can only be used, in practice, against very weak countries: war with a serious opponent would lead to a level of American casualties that the US public would not tolerate for long. And the world does not *need* America in the same sense that it did when totalitarian communist powers controlled the heart of Eurasia. But neither does it need America to go into a gigantic sulk about its lost status.

It is hard for any country to come to terms with a loss of power. Spain, the superpower of the sixteenth and early seventeenth centuries, took more than three centuries to get over the shock of losing its leading place in Europe. France, the dominant European power for the latter half of the seventeenth century and all of the eighteenth, had pretty much overcome its bitterness by the latter part of the twentieth century – say, a century and a half to recover. Britain, the superpower of the nineteenth century, has made a quicker recovery, but its consistent attempts to "punch above its weight" in international affairs by hitching a ride on America's coattails suggest that it has not fully come to terms with its real status yet. How long will America take? Nobody knows, but the course of the next fifty years will be determined in large part by how well or how badly Americans cope with the change.

The particular problem for Americans who have to make this adjustment is that they are quite unaccustomed to thinking of the United States as simply a large, English-speaking democracy with considerable ethnic diversity that occupies the middle band of the North American continent. American nationality has always been defined in ideological terms, and pretty sweeping ones at that: the cradle of democracy, to begin with, but latterly also the head office of the perfect economic system: free-market capitalism. Letting go of these illusions is bound to be painful, and there are powerful interests in Washington and elsewhere that will fight hard to keep them alive. They may not win; but if they do, Iraq will just be the first stage of a very rough ride.

Other Serpent's Tail titles of interest

TechGnosis

Erik Davis

From the printing press to the telegraph, through radio, TV and the Internet, *TechGnosis* explores the mystical impulses that lie behind our obsession with information technology.

In this thrilling book, writer and cyber guru Erik Davis demonstrates how religious imagination, magical dreams and millennialist fervour have always permeated the story of technology. Through shamanism to gnosticism, voodoo to alchemy, Buddhism to evangelism, *TechGnosis* peels away the rational shell of info tech to reveal the utopian dreams, alien obsessions and apocalyptic visions that populate the ongoing digital revolution.

'A most informative account of a culture whose secular concerns continue to collide with their supernatural flip side' Sadie Plant, *TLS*

'Beautifully written, carefully conceived and absolutely accessible, *TechGnosis* proves that it's time we sat up and took notice' *Observer*

'*TechGnosis* is a masterpiece of informed polemic, welding seemingly disparate blocs of knowledge and thought into a coherent, challenging whole with passion, erudition and wit' *Independent*

Erik Davis has written for *Wired, The Village Voice* and *Gnosis*, and he has lectured internationally on techno-culture and the fringes of religion.

What Next

A Memoir Toward World Peace
Walter Mosley

Starting with a personal memory of his father, Leroy's, war experiences, Walter Mosley writes passionately about the need for black people to become active in the struggle for world peace. He argues that because of their experience of oppression black people are crucially placed to build bridges between the affluent first world and the impoverished third world.

Based on the personal insights that are the hallmark of his fiction, *What Next* is Walter Mosley's moving call to action, a generous book that reminds us that we are all part of a wider community of interests that requires nurturing and support.

'While he may have intended it to be an "address to African America," Mosley's words will resonate with any American who questions our government's geopolitical motives and methods in these unsettling times' *LA Times*

Walter Mosley is the author of over twenty critically acclaimed books and his work has been translated into twenty-one languages. His popular mystery series featuring Easy Rawlins began with *Devil in A Blue Dress* in 1990, which was later made into a film starring Denzel Washington. Born and raised in Los Angeles, he now lives in New York.

A Time for Machetes

The Rwandan Genocide - The Killers Speak

Jean Hatzfeld

In April-May 1994 in Rwanda, 800,000 Rwandan Tutsis were massacred by their Hutu fellow citizens – more than 10,000 a day, mostly being hacked to death by machete. Jean Hatzfeld reports on the results of his interviews with nine of the Hutu killers, all of who are now in prison, some awaiting execution. Hatzfeld elicits extraordinary testimony from these men about the genocide they perpetrated. Each describes what it was like the first time he killed someone, what he felt like when he killed a mother and child, and how he reacted when he killed a cordial acquaintance. Each reflects on his feelings of moral responsibility, his guilt, remorse, or indifference to the crimes.

Since the Holocaust, it has been conventional to presume that only depraved and monstrous evil incarnate could perpetrate such crimes, but it may be, Hatzfeld suggests, that such actions are within the realm of ordinary human conduct. To read this disturbing, enlightening and very brave book is to consider the foundation of human morality and ethics in a new light.

'Hatzfeld's harrowing documentation of the voices of Rwandan killers reminds us once again how perfectly human it can be to be perfectly inhumane' Philip Gourevitch

Into the Quick of Life

The Rwandan Genocide - The Survivors Speak
Jean Hatzfeld

In Rwanda in 1994, five out of six Tutsis (800,000) were hacked to death with machetes by their Hutu neighbours. In the villages of Nyamata and N'tarama, where, in the first two days of the genocide, over 10,000 Tutsis were massacred in the churches where they sought refuge, Jean Hatzfeld interviewed some of the survivors.

Of all ages, coming from different walks of life, from orphan teenage farmers to the local social worker, fourteen survivors talk of the genocide, the death of family and friends in the church and in the marshes of Bugesera to which they fled. They also talk of their present life and try to explain and understand the reasons behind the extermination. These horrific accounts of life at the very edge contrast with Hatzfeld's own sensitive and vivid descriptions of Rwanda's villages and countryside in peacetime. *Into the Quick of Life* brings us, in the author's own words, 'as close to (the event) as we can ever get'.

'Very rarely does journalism transform itself into a work of litera-ture, that reportage and the investigation transcend the subject of the investigation: Jean Hatzfeld has achieved this miracle. His secret is his profound humanity, his persistent, almost desperate desire to find and hear all words of the human being - victim or killer. In this way, he discovers what they have in common: like us, they are ordi-nary human beings' Gil Courtemanche

'This harrowing work in its entirety is surely among the most powerful pieces of journalism of our generation' *Herald*

'*Into the Quick of Life*, Hatzfeld's second book, tells the stories of the Tutsi survivors of the genocide. It is as compelling a read. Sad, bewildered, pathetic people who lost kith and kin - often because they thought only of saving themselves. They are trying hard to forget, while forgiveness is an alien notion. A decade on, victim and perpetrator are still frozen in those 100 days the world ignored' *The Irish Independent*

Born in Madagascar in 1949, novelist and journalist Jean Hatzfeld worked for several years as foreign correspondent for French daily newspaper *Libération*, covering both the conflict in Yugoslavia, where he was wounded by machine-gun fire in 1992, and the Rwandan genocide. He lives in Paris.